KABUL CAFE

'Riveting reportage from a Canadian foreign correspondent who lived in Afghanistan off and on from 2007 to 2011. It's episodic, certainly, but also highly evocative. Most compelling of all is its cast of characters: all-American guy Jenner, trying to get his hands on 913 Kalashnikovs; Dunia, the cleaning woman who hates cleaning but has eight siblings; and Hasina, the revolutionary girl in the Gucci sunglasses. Forget all you think you know about Afghanistan, read this, and then think again.'

Caroline Sanderson,
The Bookseller

'This is war ... but not as we know it. This is not the Afghanistan you see on the news, or even in earnest "human interest" documentaries. Only Heidi would wander around Kabul in stilettos and lip-gloss, and only Heidi would come back with stories like these – the kind of stories that female war-zone journalists might whisper to their closest girlfriends, not the kind they normally publish. Heidi is sharp, funny, utterly irreverent, often poignant and always entertaining.'

Kate Fox,
author of *Watching the English*

'This wonderful cocktail of images and impressions is far more than the sum of its parts. For it offers a deep draught of the awful excitement of living on the edge of somebody else's war. An experience that no Westerner in Afghanistan would want to have missed, or to repeat.'

Sir Sherard Cowper-Coles,
former British ambassador to Afghanistan

'This is a letter from the deeply bizarre world of the "internationals", the people who gave us the disaster that is Afghanistan and who will soon move on to a disaster zone near you. Kingstone brings us into the heart of this world of misfits, creeps, rich dilettantes as well as the occasional genuine humanitarian. If you want to know what went so badly wrong in Afghanistan, read this book.'

Frank Ledwidge,
author of *Losing Small Wars* and *Investment in Blood*

'So many of the books about Afghanistan are either bloodless treatises on military strategy or sentimental stories of Afghan peasant life. Heidi Kingstone provides something more nuanced: detailed, insightful, complex stories about how surreal life can be for women in the heart of central Asia, under the overlapping influences of medieval jihad and 21st-century moneyed Western do-goodism. Not one reporter in a hundred would have the courage to traipse around Afghanistan collecting stories like these.'

Jonathan Kay, editor of *The Walrus*

ABOUT THE AUTHOR

Heidi Kingstone is a foreign correspondent with wide experience covering human rights issues, conflict and politics. She has written for Britain's leading publications, including the *Financial Times*, *The Times*, *The Sunday Times*, the *Spectator*, the *Guardian* and the *Mail on Sunday*.

Her commitment to reporting important and neglected stories has taken her to some of the most desperate places on the planet. She has covered disease and poverty from Mali to Sierra Leone; life in Darfur; and water wars between Palestine and Israel. Canada's *National Post* commissioned her to write a four-part series on the 'Worst Places in the World'. She has also written extensively on Iraq, where she travelled to Baghdad, Basra and Kurdistan.

From 2007 until 2011, Heidi lived and worked in Afghanistan.

www.HeidiKingstone.com

Dispatches
from the
Kabul Café

HEIDI KINGSTONE

Published by Advance Editions 2015

Advance Editions is an imprint of Core Q Ltd

Global House, 1 Ashley Avenue, Epsom, Surrey KT18 5AD

All correspondence: info@AdvanceEditions.com

First published as an advance ebook by Advance Editions 2014

ISBN 978-1-910408-03-2

Printed and bound in Great Britain by Clays Ltd, St Ives plc

Designed and typeset by K.DESIGN, Somerset

www.AdvanceEditions.com

For my parents

Kabul, where the odds are good,
but the goods are odd

Contents

Abbreviations

ADC	Aide-de-camp
COIN	Counterinsurgency
EVAW	Elimination of Violence against Women
FARC	The Revolutionary Armed Forces of Colombia
FOB	Forward operating base
IED	Improvised explosive device
IRS	Internal Revenue Service
ISAF	International Security Assistance Force
KAF	Kandahar Airfield
KBR	Kellogg Brown & Root, subsidiary of American procurement giant Halliburton
NATO	North Atlantic Treaty Organization
NGO	Non-governmental organization
PRT	Provincial reconstruction team
PSD	Personal security detail
PX	Post Exchange (US Army shop)
RAWA	Revolutionary Association of Women of Afghanistan

UNAMA	United Nations Assistance Mission in Afghanistan
UNHCR	United Nations High Commissioner for Refugees
UNOCA	United Nations Office for the Coordination of Humanitarian and Economic Assistance Programmes Relating to Afghanistan

Chronology

1979 Soviet invasion of Afghanistan

1980 Mujahideen backed by US, Pakistan, China, Iran and Saudi Arabia

1989 Soviet troops leave Afghanistan, civil war breaks out

1996 Taliban seize control of Kabul

2001 US-led bombing of Afghanistan begins

2005 Warlords and strongmen form majority in new Parliament

2014 NATO combat mission over and drawdown complete

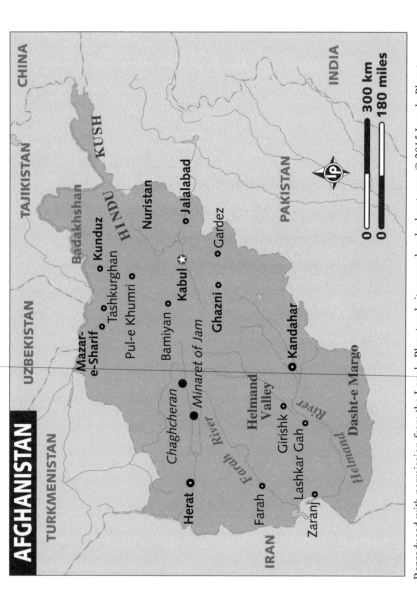

1. Introduction

There are rare moments in life when the planets align.

For me, this was my time in Afghanistan. There was nowhere else I could have been.

As a journalist, there was also no more exciting story – at times I filed articles that virtually wrote themselves; the words just spilled out. And personally, I encountered people who changed my life.

My first impression when I arrived on a miserable February day was of a city covered in mud. It felt primitive and shocking – like being transported back to the Stone Age. It was difficult to distinguish anything at all, so when people talked of the good life in the seventies, of the parties and the houses, I found it impossible to believe them. Even pictures of that period seemed unreal. But as I spent time there, and the early spring brought a thaw and flowers started to bloom, the city unfolded, and I began to see what once was, and the tarnished beauty that was still there. I had no idea then what a hold the country would come to have over me; like so many others down the centuries, I would become bewitched.

By the time I arrived, NATO had already been in Afghanistan for six years, trying to bring peace and stability and to rebuild the country.

This is where my story begins.

2. Because

In the end, I left for the same reason I went.

Because of women.

Because, like everyone else, I wanted to change things: change how women were treated, change their opportunities, change the laws, change their lives. Make their lives better. Not worse.

Because, like just about everyone else, from emperors to generals, we went in with hope. And, like everyone else, the Afghans had hope too.

Because there is always hope in the beginning; though by the end there was none.

Because, like everyone else – Afghan, American, Afghan-American – we asked why. Why didn't it work? What didn't work? How could we have made it work?

Because we built schools that had no teachers to teach. Because we built buildings that weren't needed. Because money that was allocated had to be spent – it didn't matter how. Because there was so much duplication. Because of corruption and warlords and Karzai and drugs. Because we didn't prepare for a long war. Because we cannot nation-build . . .

Because we made up stories about Afghan women – that they are the power in the house, while the men rule outside. And because Female Empowerment Teams were created based on those erroneous assumptions, so that female soldiers would be able to access and engage with Afghan women, helping them to influence home and community. But the real story is that they have no power. Inside or out.

And because we upheld another myth – that Afghan women are all sisters, united under the burqa, under the shared mantle of oppression. As if they are different from us, rather than just like us. As if there is no rivalry.

Because it made sense. To us who had no clue about Afghanistan, about its culture, about the vast differences. Who wouldn't want equal rights – human rights? Who could think it is OK to hold a young woman's feet over a fire, then dump her outside in the bitter winter night, shoeless, without a coat and with nowhere to go? Or cut girls' noses off? Or marry off child brides to old men? Or give women away to settle debts, like chattel?

2. BECAUSE

Because it changed the way I think. Challenged my morality.

Because I gave what I could – money, clothes, friendship; but not what I wanted – a better life, better options, a passport, a plane ticket, a way out, happiness, calm . . .

Because I had to leave. Like a rat on a sinking ship. Gone. Goodbye.

Because, like everyone now asks, what are we doing there?

And because, like everyone else, I still don't know.

3. It Must be Pomegranate Season Soon

I know something Ariana doesn't know. Something she should know. Something I can't tell her. I know it as she chooses the present from a shop on Chicken Street where we often browse. I know it as she picks up a solid polished rock of amethyst and I know it when I tell her I can't take it back to London; I make up an excuse and say it's too heavy. I can't let her spend so much money, almost $100, on something I know will be tossed away and abandoned – like her, as if she has no value – and I know it as she chooses a lump of lapis lazuli instead. The truth is, I know that he is not coming back for her even before I meet Ariana – even before I go to Afghanistan. I know this is something that will wreck her life. And I know I need to be there when she finds out. To explain. Yet what she doesn't know keeps her alive. This hope, this illusion of hope, is her lifeline.

In the months before I leave for Afghanistan I hear many stories about Ariana from Brian, but they revolve around what he should do about their 'relationship', his feelings of guilt and obligation and confusion. He doesn't want to marry her, never did, so what I never hear is how he loves her, or even what he likes about her. They barely speak the same language and have nothing in common. Least of all a future.

This dream that Ariana has, this thing that keeps her alive, is the idea that Brian will rescue her, as he promised. That he will take her from Kabul and marry her. That he will set her free. His irrelevant fling – a meaningless flirtation – has already altered the structure of her life. Yet regardless of what he says, his actions – to me, at least – speak loud and clear: instead of an engagement ring or an airline ticket, he has sent her a suitcase of cheap clothes, which I bring from London. He has cast her aside.

This is what I know when Ariana and I are shopping on Chicken Street. He is not coming back and he never had any intention of coming back. Why should I have to be the bearer of this news – to tell her that somehow life must go on, that she must forget about him and abandon her dreams in the same way that he has abandoned her? I think gloomily of her shattered hopes and the long, bleak future that stretches out ahead of her.

The first time I met Ariana she was painting the sharpened nails of a client. She had looked up and a sense of hostility seemed to emanate from deep inside her, a sneer spreading across her face and beneath her skin. In other circumstances I would have been polite and left. She was contemptuous and bitchy and, quite frankly, I was not sure I liked her. But then there was the sisterhood and this was Afghanistan – and that involved a self-imposed sense of duty. I also felt a certain loyalty to Brian, and a misplaced sense of responsibility for Ariana. But Ariana was not entirely the tragic operatic innocent left behind by her lover; she was a woman who desperately wanted out, and Brian was her passport.

In London we'd talked of little else except what he should do about the Ariana situation.

'I think you need to bring her here,' I told him at his rented flat near Notting Hill. 'You don't have to marry her, but get her out of the country.'

During all our discussions, I wondered to myself whether I should offer to help, be less selfish, practise what I preached. Perhaps, I thought, she could stay with me, and I could support her while she adjusted to a new life and learned more English, because if I were in the same situation, I would want someone to help me.

'She could have the spare room,' he mused. But he didn't really want the responsibility. And what a huge one it would be. He would have to house her, bolster her, be her foundation, carry her weight. How that would have cramped his style. Besides, in a few months, his job would take him to somewhere in the South Pacific, on another mission, to another life.

Nevertheless, the game continued, and the further away I got from Brian and Britain, the more I wondered why we were friends, although I knew that wasn't fair. He was smart and interesting, well travelled and knowledgeable, but my anger and disappointment took hold, because this was not the West and the rules here were different. Casual affairs with Afghan women have consequences, and I cannot imagine what went through his head as he pursued this doomed encounter. What did he think when they were alone together, knowing the social norms of Afghan society and knowing too that she would never fit into his life? Did he care so little that he would let her suffer the inevitable, frightening consequences? Was he so caught up in a whirlwind of love and romance? In the end, the only reasonable conclusion I could draw was that his vanity overtook his sanity.

Brian always maintained the relationship was Ariana's initiative, which it might well have been, but so what? He should have known better because, of course, the nights of sex, if that is indeed what they were, turned to talk of marriage. But he never wanted to marry her, and knew when he left that he wouldn't. Still, he could never bring himself to tell her. So when he was posted back home, he stalled. He told her it was difficult to get her a visa; that he was trying, but dealing with his government was proving tricky. He said he couldn't meet her because of work constraints. He said he couldn't return to Afghanistan owing to safety restrictions so instead he called and lulled her into a false sense of security. He palmed her off with excuses that anyone who wasn't desperate could have seen through, and this went on for two years, until I met her in the winter of 2007.

A single woman's life in Kabul is not the fun and independent existence enjoyed in the West, and after work Ariana can't just ring up one of her mates and say, 'Hey, let's grab a pizza and go to a movie.' Firstly, she doesn't have any mates: her colleagues at the salon don't much like her and their husbands are suspicious of her 'bad influence'. She has to be home by 6 p.m., alone, in her empty flat with random electricity, no TV and often no heat in the harsh winter months, otherwise people will talk. Talk costs lives. Neighbours, colleagues, men, women, have already branded her a prostitute – an easy but deadly accusation. Young women, women in general, don't live alone, away from family, without a man for protection.

As part of my sisterhood campaign, I have taken her out – for coffee, on shopping expeditions and one time for dinner at Le Bistro, an expat hangout. Quite honestly, each moment we were there was painfully eked out. I felt the seconds ticking by, astonished at how long a second could be, willing the evening to end quickly. There was this air about Ariana that nothing was quite good enough and her haughtiness put me on edge.

We spoke haltingly to each other in English: mine is pretty good, but Ariana has not yet mastered it. On the other hand, her Dari is pretty good, and mine is non-existent. She managed to let me know that she didn't like the vol-au-vent she'd asked me to order. She poked it quite violently with her fork as it sat helplessly and blamelessly on her plate. The vol-au-vent was also something I wanted to rescue. She irritated me.

In local Afghan restaurants women sit, shunted in a corner, apart from men (who eat in the main space), tucked away from view, from unwarranted stares, from prying eyes. In the Kabul-posh French restaurant, where beautiful kilims hang from the walls, we ate together at a square table covered by a starched white linen cloth with fresh spring flowers in a small, deep-blue, handmade Herat glass vase.

Herat, famous for its glasswork, borders Iran, where Ariana grew up. Like millions of Hazaras, the Shia Muslim descendants of Genghis Khan, her family fled when the Soviets came, when civil war broke out in the 1990s, when the Sunni Taliban took power later that decade. But since the overthrow of Mullah Omar and his government, many Afghan refugees have returned home.

Only in Ariana's case, the return was not her choice. She had worked as a nanny for a foreign family in Tehran, and when they were posted abroad they wanted her to join them. As an undocumented Afghan in Iran, she needed to go back to Afghanistan, a country she hadn't seen in more than thirty years, to acquire an identity. But while she was in Kabul, on what was meant to be a brief stay, the husband of the family she worked for lost his job. Ariana was stranded.

She'd hated Iran, where Afghans were referred to as dogs, and she hated Afghanistan too – a country full of dirty, illiterate peasants, she said. Ariana wanted out (before she went out of her mind) – anywhere would be better than this backward hellhole. Then she met Brian.

When I talk about Brian, Ariana blushes and is coy. I tell her what he says, which in this case is true: 'He cannot return to Afghanistan.' (He could, of course, meet her in India or Pakistan or Dubai – all places Afghans can go without too much hassle.) Still, I continue with my reams of excuses, interjecting as we talk that she must think of other things, must make alternative plans – just in case. I can see the tears welling up. I cannot do this.

When finally I no longer know what to do, what to say – when I am frustrated by Brian's lack of decency or transparency about his holiday romance in hell, by his refusal to call her or to return her calls, I ask my Kabul friends for help.

We all want to come up with solutions, to find options for Ariana, and make her realize she cannot wait for Brian or rely on him to rescue her. We suggest ways to improve her English; we offer to pay for lessons so she can find better employment than working as a beautician, but my worry is that she might kill herself when she finally acknowledges that the small line of hope has been withdrawn and she has been cast adrift with no life raft.

My ability to help is limited, genuinely constrained by legal and financial parameters and, possibly, emotional ones too. Ariana has unrealistic expectations and thinks I should be able to work miracles. She thinks I should be able to get her a visa to Canada, take her to Pakistan (because Afghan women aren't allowed to travel alone) or find her a job in the UK. I don't tell her, but I have left my magic wand behind.

I try, but I'm going in circles, spiralling downwards, down to the centre of the earth.

But there is always hope.

It is Afghan New Year, Nawruz, the first day of spring, and to celebrate Ariana and I plan an outing. Life must go on.

The traffic is terrible when Fahim and I pick Ariana up. The roads are chaotic; mobs of people are out celebrating. Men in vans sing and dance, listening to outrageously loud music, dizzy on the excitement or possibly on the drugs produced here. Near the university, in the district where Ariana lives, police have blocked the roads with juggernauts, a security precaution. It takes forever to negotiate a way out. At the back of everyone's mind is the possibility of being trapped in this mess if a bomb goes off.

Once we get clear of the crowds and are off, past the little shops where blue wigs on mannequins match flammable blue dresses and long pink tresses match dreadful flamingo-pink outfits, past an open-air school under the cover of a UN tarpaulin, the conversation grows animated. Fahim is busy translating from English to Dari and back.

Fahim is a doctor I met while I was doing an interview

with female drug users for a magazine. After we discussed addiction, he kindly offered to take me for an afternoon drive out of Kabul so that I might see some of the countryside, and I'd asked Ariana if she would like to join us. I wonder if Fahim and Ariana will like each other, even though I know this is not how things are done in Afghanistan – men and women don't date – and Fahim no doubt has a wife and family.

Out of the denseness of the capital, idyllic green fields and fresh rushing streams stretch before us. Afghanistan is beautiful. 'This is where I would build a house if I stayed here,' Ariana comments. Do I see a spark or is it only my imagination? I want things to work out for her. I want Ariana to find happiness and security, and I look at her and at Fahim and know nothing will happen.

Leaving behind the oppression of Kabul, the dusty air, the grittiness, a momentary respite has to be good for Ariana as much as for me. Everything seems fun and normal and light-hearted. The weather is magical, and I am falling more and more in love with this country. As the day comes to an end, just before sunset, I am sorry to drop Ariana back home. When the car door shuts, the harsh grind of daily reality seems to begin again.

***

Then, one night soon after, reality really does kick in. Ariana calls me, hysterical. Someone is going to kill her, she says. I don't understand. She is crying, begging me for help. I hardly know the landscape of the country. I don't know what to do. She calls me again – every few minutes, each time more and more frenzied, telling me I need to get her out of her apartment.

The only thing I can think of is to call a South African I had met a couple of days earlier at a makeshift club in someone's house – more like a speakeasy, really, both literally and metaphorically underground. People there were dancing, but Dave had been sitting at the bar and we'd started to talk. He had told me he was a doctor (more like a witch doctor, I thought), but that he'd given it up to start a nightclub in Kabul. He also said he was ex-Special Forces. (Every mercenary and every ex-soldier claimed to be ex-Special Forces; few actually were.) At some point during the evening he'd pulled up his polo shirt to show me the tattoo on his back – a devil with a pitchfork and a cheeky smile. It made me nauseous. We'd exchanged numbers, although I couldn't imagine we would ever see each other again. But then this was Kabul and you just never knew.

So I call Dave and tell him as much as I have been able to establish: that there is this panicked Afghan woman being threatened by someone and that he has to help her. I give him the address and her phone number, then call Ariana back and say assistance is on the way.

Dave calls later to say he is with 'his men' and has rescued Ariana, collected her clothes and whatever documents she has. He tells me that the landlord was screaming at them as they left. Then everything goes quiet.

Dave takes Ariana to his house and makes her turn off her phone, so that she can't be traced. For days I lose touch with her. Dave never answers his phone, which makes me crazy, but at least he calls back. I think he is being ridiculous.

Now that Ariana is safely installed in Dave's villa, I have time to ask myself who is this man who saved her. And what has he saved her from? I can only partially answer these questions. It seems she rejected the advances of an Afghan man she knew. These were persistent and unpleasant but, up until now, manageable. The situation changed, however, when she told him she hated him and found him repulsive. Ariana is now considered fair game.

Weeks pass and I barely hear from Ariana or Dave, except on occasion to let me know all is OK. But I have a sense that something is brewing when Dave says Ariana follows him around like a star-struck teenager. This would be an unusual ending, and I wonder if they might fall in love.

The next call I get from Dave is to tell me he has work in Helmand, and that Ariana will have to leave the villa. We are back to square one: he doesn't believe the threat has abated; he thinks she needs to leave the country. I insist that he and I meet, and he suggests L'Atmosphère. We can sit in the garden there, he says, and figure out what to do. He is not worried that anyone will overhear him.

He has a plan.

'I am going to take Ariana by donkey over the mountains to Pakistan,' he says.

'Oh, great. Along the well-worn drug-smuggling route,' I reply acerbically. I am dumbfounded and now actively worried about Dave's mental stability.

Brian is suddenly back in the loop. He suggests Ariana returns to Iran, where she can live with her parents, and he has offered to cover the cost of the ticket. For him this is the most sensible, and possibly only, solution. He may be right, but she is having none of it. Dave prepares for Helmand, leaving Ariana alone in the house. It is during this time that she calls me, crying uncontrollably. She is still worried that this leering man, bent on revenge for his thwarted sexual advances, is going to kill her. This is all so dramatic, and with the backdrop of Afghanistan still relatively new to me I have no idea how much of it is real.

Luckily, a more sensible plan falls into place, and that is to get Ariana to India. There, she can be with her sister who lives in Delhi; she can work as a beautician and start afresh. People who hardly know Ariana – friends of her employer – generously offer to help.

For a while, peace and calm prevail and all seems to be well.

Then I get a call from Ariana's sister in India. 'My sister is going to die,' she cries. 'They are going to kill my sister. You have to help save her life.'

'I am doing everything I possibly can,' I tell her, and wonder how, of all the people in Afghanistan and Iran, I have assumed this responsibility.

Despite knowing that the cause is not only lost but stupid, I end up trailing from one embassy to another, feeling like a complete idiot, pursuing a doomed mission. The Americans just laugh when I explain Ariana's situation – that she once worked for an American woman who had tried to get her a visa but in the end had failed. They hoot as they tell me she is like millions of others and will have to join the queue.

I can only stand so much humiliation and rejection in a day, and for a bit of respite before we trek to yet another embassy, I take Ariana for tea at the Serena. It's

Afghanistan's only five-star hotel and I think it might cheer us both up. It really is beautiful, with its elegant landscaped gardens, pergolas, graceful fountains, long walkways, and outdoor swimming pool.

Traditionally dressed and turbaned guards greet guests as they open the intricately carved wooden double doors that lead onto the lobby, which overlooks two outdoor terraces. Armchairs and settees, covered in the reds and blues and browns of Afghan fabrics, are serenely set around Afghan rugs and low, carved tables. The mountains frame every image in Kabul and their peaks provide a dramatic backdrop to the wide expanse of green lawns. The three-storey hotel is modern, clean, calm and alcohol-free. The Friday brunches are lavish, with a wide array of food, from sushi to pasta, which often looks better than it tastes, but you can't help but be impressed. The Aga Khan Fund for Economic Development, which has restored and managed this venture, has done a remarkable job. As time passes the security gets tighter and tighter, and the Serena itself comes under numerous fatal attacks.

In all fairness, I don't think Ariana knows what to expect; she has an air of worldliness about her, but in reality her world is very small. I understand why Brian couldn't marry her.

She has bought me a scarf, a transparent black one with colourful embroidery, because I'd said previously I liked one that she was wearing. I want her to find a way out.

Our next stop is the Canadian embassy. These are my people, but when I go to register they are not particularly hospitable, leaving us out on the empty, barricaded street. It is cordoned off, a guard sitting in a shack on the dusty road. Ariana fills in the forms, and when we finally get inside they tell us that she must go to Pakistan to apply for a visa. I knew all this before, but am going through the pointless motions for some intangible reason, which no doubt stems from guilt and a genuine inability to effect any change. I don't think she realizes what a hopeless pursuit this is; people have made promises to her, and she has believed them. Rather like the promises international governments made to Afghans, and the Afghan government made to its own people.

At UNHCR, they tell her she cannot apply for asylum in her own country and that she must do it from a third state. I feel as if I am caught up in some Kafkaesque scenario with nowhere to turn. Every possible path leads to another dead end and so we return to plotting and planning Ariana's Afghan exit.

Ariana does eventually make it to India, but only for a few months, after which time her visa expires. She doesn't like the Indians; she doesn't like the accommodation; she doesn't find any suitable work. Nothing is good enough. 'It's dirty,' she says, and she is happy to leave, even if it means coming back to Kabul.

And now it is my turn to decamp.

I am due in London. I can do no more for Ariana.

On the day of my departure the sun shines as usual, the donkey carts heave under the weight of fruit and vegetables – oranges, watermelons, cauliflowers. Sheep heads are piled up outside shopfronts on Butcher Street; skinned animal carcasses hang from meat hooks above them, attracting as many flies as customers. Men and boys sell phone cards on the street or offer to exchange money, preferably US dollars. Women float by, their blue burqas billowing behind them – again images framed by the jagged mountain range encircling the capital. Piles of rubbish lie heaped and rotting on streets whose houses are hidden behind gates, concealing beauty as well as horror. On Flower Street, the garish plastic flowers so beloved of Afghans fill the windows. The shops on Chicken Street compete with each other to shift jewellery, rugs and clothes . . .

On the way to the airport it occurs to me that it must be pomegranate season soon. And now what I know, Ariana knows too.

4. First Days, Early Days, Crazy Days

Rewind to the beginning . . .

It is an unbelievably cold winter, just like home.

Day One

The call to prayer bellows from the mosque on the corner, waking me up with a heart-attack-inducing jolt. It is so unnervingly loud that it might as well be in the room. In fact, I wonder if it's a personal directive from above. When the sound is particularly deafening it means the electricity is working; it also wakes up the rooster somewhere outside, which crows in competition for the rest of my stay. The first call begins at about 5 a.m. and the different muezzins sing at slightly staggered times.

It's a relatively soft landing into my three-month contract with an American PR firm for which I am working as a communications specialist. The offer came about by sheer happenstance; someone recommended me for the job and I jumped at the chance to go to Afghanistan. The official interview had taken place a few weeks earlier over dinner in Dubai. Once the deal was formalized, I prepared for the mission by stockpiling lots of beauty products to combat the unforgiving climate, none of which was available at that time in Kabul, and by doing research, starting with the Economist Intelligence Unit's report on Afghanistan. Even then it cited corruption as the cancer at the centre of the country. It's a sad state of affairs that so many people have enriched themselves through illicit means. As a result many Afghans feel that there is not much to show for the one trillion dollars that will ultimately have been spent on this mission. The litany that always dogs development – lack of security, lack of human capital, corruption, drugs, the insurgency, treatment of women, illiteracy, poverty – is repeated here.

Which is why, despite the corporate gig, the journalist in me isn't dormant: I am still doing my regular weekly column for Johannesburg's *Saturday Star*, as well as quite a bit of freelance work for other publications.

When I go downstairs for breakfast in the company house I share with my workmates, I am handed delicious fresh orange juice and good coffee, the perfect way to start the day. Then I meet Minoo.

4. FIRST DAYS, EARLY DAYS, CRAZY DAYS

Everyone here has a story.

Minoo, whom we refer to as Gilda after the 1946 movie starring Rita Hayworth, is our Afghan cleaner. She is very glamorous – a feat in itself when you consider all the sartorial restraints. Today she wears a floral blouse with blue stars on a white background and a ruffle down the front. Her hair is done up and a Givenchy scarf drapes down like a genie in a bottle. The scarf is obviously a fake, not that it matters, and she probably has no idea what this iconic brand is, but she makes it look almost as elegant as Audrey Hepburn did when she was Hubert de Givenchy's muse. I tell her she looks beautiful.

Minoo has three sons. Her husband was killed years ago by the warlord Gulbuddin Hekmatyar's brutal fundamentalist Hezb-i-Islami. As a university student, Hekmatyar was known for throwing acid in the faces of unveiled women. He moved from being pro-Soviet to fighting against the Russian occupation. Then he fought the other resistance movements in the civil war that began in 1992 and left 50,000 Afghans dead. Despite being responsible for much of the terrible destruction, he became prime minister twice and then had to flee when the Taliban took over. The human side of war. Nothing in Afghanistan is ever straightforward.

I realize that in spite of carefully considered preparation, I have nothing appropriate to wear. Whatever I have brought is too short, too transparent or too tight.

The French woman I work with offers to take me shopping. I am also tasked with getting some furniture for my room, which, ultimately, takes me to Chicken Street, the central shopping drag of the capital.

Out of absolute desperation, the first things I buy are two hideous coats. They make me look like an extra from the early episodes of *Coronation Street* and I want to kill myself. Made of cheap and nasty cotton and synthetic fibres, they are shapeless with white plastic buttons – they are an affront to the senses and I dump them immediately.

I am somewhat cheered, however, when we go to check out one of Kabul's few designer shops – 'designer' is a loose concept here.

Zarif, which means 'precious' in Dari, is a clothing line started by Zolaykha Sherzad, a talented Afghan-Swiss-American woman. She left the country when she was ten, after the Soviets invaded, went on to study architecture, and later returned to Afghanistan, like so many others, once the Taliban had retreated. Her company employs women who hand-embroider and cut clothes based on traditional Afghan designs. Zolay makes jackets and coats out of beautiful silks and cottons, mostly striped, in bold, rich colours – cherry reds, royal blues, emerald greens, pinks and aristocratic purples.

They are extremely popular with the expat crowd. They are also cut for Zolaykha, who is a size 2.

While the look may be Afghan, the prices are Western – $100 for a silk shirt and multiples of that for a jacket. I'm shocked (but weeks later recover, as I realize that everything is expensive). I can't bring myself to buy anything because, quite frankly, I don't like any of it, but I do like Zolay, who is tiny and delicate, gentle and thoughtful. She is also annoying because she effortlessly switches between Dari and English and French, which is just not fair. Still, I try not to seem bitter. Her atelier is off one of the most poorly maintained roads in the city, with deep potholes that are full of water. Behind steel gates, stepping stones lead across the garden to her atelier, where the women work and the jackets, coats, blouses and scarves are displayed.

Not far from the workshop, the road leads to one of the capital's main streets, Kolola Pushta. Seeing it for the first time makes a huge impression on me. I find Kabul beautiful, exotic, unlike anything I have ever seen, full of colour, and uniquely Afghan.

Shiny silver fish bolted to white styrofoam boards glitter in the sunlight at the restaurant across from Cinema Park, made famous in Khaled Hosseini's *The Kite Runner*. Carts parked along the road sell colourful and delicious-looking produce – everything from enormous melons to grapes and aubergines, and I'm told there will be pomegranates in the autumn. Men and boys stand over their psychedelic fruit and veg and whip the dust away with long-tailed brushes. Small children sell peanuts, little girls carry home snowshoe-shaped nans almost bigger than they are, and women in burqas talk with each other in groups on the street corners. Young boys, maybe six years old, stand in between the heavy lines of congested traffic, flogging maps or pictures of Ahmad Shah Massoud and other Afghan heroes and villains. The intensity of the sun and the harshness of the climate have aged the boys' small faces, making them resemble wizened old men. And there are peacocks for sale on the street corner. Absolutely amazing!

On Chicken Street people bargain for jewels and carpets and other souvenirs, as they have done for decades. Hand-woven Afghan rugs hang outside, while indoors neat piles are stacked side by side almost to the ceiling. Scarves of varying descriptions in silks and cottons and mysterious synthetics, in bright colours and muted ones, patterned and plain, are displayed outside shops, luring in the casual consumer. If you look hard enough in the shops that sell fur, you may discover the occasional pelt of a rare and endangered snow leopard. Stores are treasure troves of traditional Afghan furniture, carved wooden tables and doors, and hand-painted chests and mirrors. Lapis lazuli in every conceivable shape and size is available, and everyone engages you in conversation and offers tea. It is always an experience.

In 2007 it is still safe enough to walk down, even for UN staff who are often under the strictest restrictions, but as the violence gets progressively worse year by year, they will be forbidden from going there. This impacts on the local shopkeepers who depend on free-spending foreigners.

I discover Mokhtar, which becomes my favourite shop. It has wonderful jewellery and artefacts and the owner speaks excellent English, learned from his years in California, home to the largest community of expat Afghans in the USA. During this first visit, two Afghan women and several bodyguards enter the shop and, in a flurry of activity, seemingly out of nowhere, bolts of fabric, placed along the glass counter top, are suddenly weighted down with elaborate jewels – thick bracelets, chandelier earrings, heavy gem-studded necklaces, and bejewelled rings. These people are big spenders.

When the entourage leaves, laden with gold and diamonds, the owner reveals that they are part of President Karzai's clan. It makes me happy to know that his money is being spent well.

Somewhere along the way I buy an emerald necklace. The stones are mined mostly in the Panjshir valley, once home to Ahmed Shah Massoud, the political and military resistance leader and national Afghan hero, who was assassinated two days before 9/11, probably by al-Qaeda. Afghanistan is blessed with deposits of almost every type of gemstone except diamonds. There are pale pink kunzites and wistful blue topazes, startlingly watery aquamarines, sulky green peridots, pink tourmalines, rosy spinels and blood-red rubies.

I learn a new word: *chapaloos* – 'ass-kissers'. I also love the sound of *ruberoo*, which means 'straight', useful when directing taxi drivers.

Day Two

Kabul's landscape is still full of ruins, skeletons of buildings, roofs caving in, bombed-out palaces – all a legacy of the civil war. There are streets of buildings with no windows, just brick edifices barely upright, defying gravity, and fallen blocks of concrete, riddled with bullet holes, and foundations of buildings that lean precariously on nothing at all.

I round a corner and come across a bizarre yet amazing sight: layers of disused buses piled high. The blue and white city buses that still work look barely roadworthy. All over the city crowds of men and women walk en masse, shopping for vegetables, stopping for tea, and the aroma wafts from the chargrilled lamb and chicken of the kebab sellers. I never become accustomed to seeing the hanging animal carcasses, especially sheep, on Butcher Street, or the knot of workers who gather on the corners in the morning waiting to be chosen as day labourers.

Flat-roofed houses fill all the available space on the mountainsides. From my window I can see the sweeping walls of the imposing fortress of Bala Hissar on the hill at the tail end of the mountain. In Macroyan, the Soviet-built enclave in the capital that was once home to the communist elite, the bleak square apartment blocks contrast with the new narcotecture: massive houses that glint in the sun. The music of the ice cream sellers in spring and summer jingles through the air throughout the capital. On TV Hill, the city's antennas stretch up to the clouds. Against a pale mud-coloured city the balloon seller walks though the streets with his extraordinary array of balloons on a stick: full, round inflated balls of pink and red, orange and blue, white and green, waiting for happy children. Every image in Kabul is a picture.

•••

The roads and pavements, which are one and the same, are completely uneven with rocks jutting out. I teeter along in my wedges – sensible shoes in London – and vow never to do this again. I can barely walk. Yet Afghan women have this miracle ability to stride along in heels – we have car-to-bar shoes; for them it's car to bazaar.

It's time to meet the team I will be working with at one of the ministries. Ministers have legions of expensive advisors who have come to show them how to run the country. I am an advisor, but in all honesty my knowledge is in journalism, which is not what they need here. Besides trying to rebuild this fractured country, everyone is trying to get their hands on the money. After thirty years of war, it's hardly surprising that institutions don't work; there is a demand for external expertise, but also for foreign money. There is an astonishing amount washing around the capital. The big contracts have lured in hustlers and hedonists, Harvard graduates and hard grafters, Afghan expats returning and foreign-born Afghans here for the first time – all spurred on by the money, adventure, a need to contribute and a sense of satisfaction. Ah, but it's not so easy.

The reason I am here is because the American company I work for needs to charge the US State Department for a three-month position that I fill. This kind of thing is not uncommon, I discover.

From the main staircase of the ministry, I can see Darul Aman Palace, the old king's residence. It must have been beautiful once, but now its emaciated edifice is like a movie-set façade, and its two tower-like structures make a heroic attempt to hold the rest of the building together before it collapses under the weight of tragic memories. The ministry is also near the National Museum, which has been rebuilt with international aid money. Under the Taliban, who destroyed any art made with a human form, brave museum staff saved many treasures by hiding them in the presidential bank vault.

My team of locals seem pretty competent and speak excellent English. The two young men grew up in Pakistan, only recently returning to a land they barely knew.

They take me to Chaila, a popular place for lunch for people from the ministry. Nearby, the French bakery in Karte Seh has great biscuits and bread. It's also an area where missionaries tend to live, and the café is said to be their hangout. Many months later, a fatal shooting takes place just outside here; for now, however, you can still get a loyalty card and a free cup of coffee.

Day Three

The Westerners I live with, English and American, have only contempt for Afghans. One shakes his head in a rage, jowls flapping, and says that you have to treat the Afghans 'like children'. Another talks about needing to keep them at a distance until they are civilized by the Brits. The worst bit is that there are Afghans in the room, listening. Is it The Great Game all over again?

The big news of the week is how the country has been thrown into a crisis because it has run out of red wine (at one point, table Chianti sells for US$75 a bottle). This is the result of the Attorney General's mini-crusade – he emptied many cellars and arrested fourteen people for selling alcohol, which is illegal. As is drinking it, of course.

I like the set-up we have at the ranch. We expat staff live in an old traditional house with a large garden. One of the highlights is that we do a lot of entertaining. About twelve people come to dinner, and the conversation yields valuable insights on Afghanistan. Our guests are a journalist from CNN, a British academic, an American writer and a diplomat.

While outside the winter temperature hovers well below zero, the powerful heaters in the dining room push the thermometer up to tropical highs. It's way too hot and getting pretty uncomfortable, and tonight is naturally the one night I have decided to wear a wool dress. At some point over dinner I glance down to see that the priceless emeralds, purchased on Chicken Street, have started to run and my rather cool and sophisticated demeanour is somewhat diminished by the green that is now dripping from the necklace and dyeing my skin.

Day Four

The first rule of PR is *never mislead*: eventually you get found out.

Journalists and PR people are not natural bedfellows. In 2007 one of the biggest issues is what is termed collateral damage – civilian casualties, innocents killed in crossfire. It has been a tug of war between the NATO ISAF press office and the corps of journalists to get reliable information.

American Vice President Dick Cheney was visiting Bagram airbase when a suicide bomb went off, killing twenty-three and injuring twenty more.

That was not supposed to happen.

ISAF claimed the number of casualties was between one and four. The Afghan Ministry of Information had accurately reported the much higher figure.

I meet a man who works for ISAF. He is oddly unable to filter his own stream of consciousness, and talks about the lying that goes on at HQ. This bothers him. He discusses the vast amounts of hardware flying above us. He reveals the accuracy of the intel and explains how it doesn't take much to liquidate a target. A phone call to NATO HQ will provide clearance and fifteen minutes later the target will have evaporated. Fascinating. I love this stuff.

Day Five

Ajmal works at the house and drives me to the office.

Before he starts his day he goes to the public baths. He could pay 20Afs (less than a penny) and share a cubicle, but he pays 50Afs instead for privacy. Running water remains a luxury for many Afghans. What has significantly changed is the access to electricity, which was non-existent before. Now the houses up and down the hills of Kabul light up the night sky.

We vary the route to work for security reasons, but pass the zoo and the psychiatric hospital. I want to visit them both.

At the entrance to the zoo is a wonderful green statue of a grinning alligator – easily the cheeriest thing there and a complete contrast to an ancient, rusty ride that creaks into motion. The latter is boat-shaped, its colours long faded, and it swings backwards and forwards, scarily high, probably only moments away from disaster. It makes a huge noise, seems immensely popular with the men and young children and would most likely be condemned almost anywhere else.

Sadder still is the old man who sits crumpled up beside an old tin car-rally toy that looks like it was manufactured in the nineteenth century. A little boy cranks the wheel to watch the car go round the circuit. Families amble by, like a day out anywhere. The aquarium is in a dusty room that has parakeets as its main display. Common fish swim in the tanks.

No grass grows anywhere, the premises are battered, but it's popular. The animals, what few there are, look sad and mangy. The monkeys have shabby fur, some are bald – none looks healthy. There is one pig and there are two porcupines. Ajmal tells me the Afghans have a saying: if you take one of the quills and put it in your house there will be fights. I have no idea what this means.

The elephant has gone, two sad lions sleep in the spring sun and one of the peacocks shows off its fantastic tail to the crowd, much to his own pleasure, no doubt. The vultures are packed into a large cage and the flock preys on one bird – birds of prey preying on a bird of prey. Its poor little heart pumps and you can see fear in its cold eyes as the largest and meanest of the mean picks at his feathers – others watch, some hold him down or pick at his wing and tail feathers. He doesn't stand much chance. I have to leave. I'm sure there are analogies to make, but they seem too obvious. Nearby, the mini waterfall flows into the polluted and practically drained Kabul River.

Next up, the psychiatric hospital. There isn't much in the way of mental-health care or qualified professionals in Afghanistan. It is usually my express purpose to avoid hospitals anywhere in the world, for any and all reasons. I hate them. I take a passing interest in mental illness, which I come by reasonably honestly as my father is a psychiatrist. Even though psychopathy is still stigmatized, it is also oddly trendy now in the West; everyone seems to be either bipolar, depressed or dependent on Prozac.

Dr Qureshi is the lone psychiatrist in the hospital compound, and one of the few in the country. At first he is reluctant to talk to either me or Ajmal, or even to let us in, but Ajmal's powers of persuasion clearly sway him. He invites us into his small office, where he offers us green tea and boiled sweets.

Qureshi was trained in Pakistan, where he worked for many years before deciding to come back home. He says he gets paid $50 a month, not a salary that many people find attractive. He explains that he wants to contribute to his country.

Just as I am preparing to leave, Dr Qureshi offers to show us around. Having missed out on the medical gene, I've seen enough and try to make my excuses, but Ajmal wants to take the tour and I am too polite to say no. Sombre and silent, the corridors are dark and dismal. The tiny cots are dirty and all pushed together. It hardly seems like a place in which to recover. Dr Qureshi's patients suffer from bipolar disorder and many are just plain depressives. The only female – an eighteen-year-old girl – lies in a cavernous, deserted ward, visited by relatives who stand solemnly by her bed.

There are many reasons to be depressed in this country. Yet the irony is that for me, and people like me, it is a place that makes us feel so alive. I cannot wait for the tour to end.

Day Six

My French colleague and I turn out to have more to talk about than just clothes.

I have reached a point, early in my stay, where I feel physically sick when I overhear conversations about people knowing each other from the disaster circuit – people who met in the former Yugoslavia, East Timor, Baghdad – and I begin to dread the words, 'When I was in . . .'

But it is not surprising, given that my colleague has been on the disaster circuit for many years, that she and I have a mutual friend – an infamous (or famous, depending on your point of view) mercenary who was previously in the British military.

I figure pretty early on, soon after we meet in fact, that she must know '007'. I know somehow that the topic will eventually arise, not least because I will ensure that it does.

Being wildly indiscreet and comparing notes with her turns out to be huge fun but not nearly as much fun as visiting the Serena Hotel with her and walking straight into the man himself. You could not make this up.

For someone who has legendary nerves of steel, he looks rather shaken and stirred as the two of us approach him.

After uncomfortable greetings and insincere pleasantries all around, we try to disengage as quickly as possible.

He says: 'I'm here to see the troops.'

The bags under his eyes are baggier than ever.

Pause.

'So am I!' I so desperately want to cry out. But don't.

Which I regret to this day.

Day Seven

Rumours are rife. The plot of the day is that President Karzai will be overthrown. The British and the Americans are apparently in on it: they want rid of him – Karzai is weak, and he is no longer playing their game. It is also said that he has stashed pots of money in secret accounts because he knows the Americans won't protect him when his time runs out. Do any Afghan leaders survive once their term in office is over, people ask.

I am, not much later, obliged to report that he is still alive and still well and still president.

Gossip Girl

A key issue at this point in the War on Terror is the different roles performed by the various NATO countries. The Canadians, the Brits, the Dutch, the Danes and the Americans are in the centre of the battle, at the forefront of war-fighting. The Germans, the French and the Swedes are much derided by everyone, as they are not allowed to venture too far from base (for many reasons, including their own rules of engagement). Popular lore has it they are too busy sunbathing. I am happy to spread the rumours.

I am also propagating the (patently untrue) myth that the Americans helicopter members of the Taliban to other parts of the country in order to expand and extend the war for their own benefit.

March 2007

It is spring.

I meet Fahim at the clinic he runs, for my story on women and drugs. The house is on the outskirts of the city, up winding dirt roads that climb higher and higher and lead past several graveyards. It's not a salubrious part of town. The opium poppy grown in Helmand province fuels drug addiction in the West, but its narcotic derivative is also used here for many ailments – it's often added to tea to help with back pain and even to calm babies.

Fahim and I make a plan to drive to the Shomali plain, where there was fierce fighting during the Soviet occupation and the subsequent civil war. In parts of the desolate and wide valley, lives are lived in low, flat compounds behind mud walls that shroud village life. Outside, women in burqas gather with their children at gravesites. Their purple haze reminds me of flowering jacarandas.

On the other side of the road, a huddle of men wait for two burly dogs to commence a brutal fight. One villager motions for us to come closer, and points to an empty parking space. I really don't care to see a dogfight, and when it begins I look away. There is nothing else for me to do but leave.

Just before we arrive in Jalalabad, there is a fish restaurant right on the water where we stop and have lunch. It's a beautiful if rickety setting, and I am taking my chances with the food, despite having already had one episode of being sicker than I have ever been. I have come to regard this as my Afghan weight-loss plan.

This outing is my first experience of the countryside and is one of my strongest memories. Afghanistan is more than just weapons, women and warlords. Amazingly, I am not felled by any malevolent bacteria.

It is around this time that my stint with the PR firm comes to an end, only six weeks after I arrive in Kabul. Office politics, even in the graveyard of empires. This works in my favour – I am writing like a djinn has taken hold of me, and words just pour out (luckily in fully formed sentences and paragraphs).

The city is full of rogues and miscreants, but what is truly fascinating are the incredibly smart, ambitious, and creative people at the top of their game – from journalists to aid workers, diplomats and many others – who have also landed here. Afghanistan is the culmination of all my professional aspirations as a foreign correspondent, and I embrace it wholeheartedly.

5. Nine Hundred Kalashnikovs

Finding 900 Kalashnikovs is no easy task, even in a place like Kabul.

Spring 2011

When Jenner, an American friend, asked if he could leave something at the house, I said, 'OK.' He promised it was only for a few days, and I had no problem with that. I didn't need more of an explanation, although in retrospect, I probably should have asked.

Later the same day he brought two long, fat tubes wrapped in brown paper and, helped by two guards who had two legs between them, he put the mysterious packages in the little hut at the front of the house.

That is how I came to be in possession of two rocket-propelled grenades.

Winter 2005

When the door of the plane finally opened, the freezing air cut right through Jenner's bones; the chill did not leave him for several years. Kabul airport, thought Jenner, was a dilapidated eyesore of a building, a miserable place people passed through as quickly as possible to escape to another country. The only illumination in the dark, gutted bowels of this sad heap of bricks revealed dangling electrical wires, the scars of scavenging for anything that could be sold for scrap. The single carousel lay silent, sabotaged by baggage handlers who pilfered through the pyramid of international luggage, stealing goods that were easily flogged on the black market.

After waiting in a long queue to clear customs and immigration, and finally retrieving his own bags, Jenner found his driver and headed to the Mustafa – then the only hotel in town and the original journalists' hangout. When huge amounts of foreign capital began to pour into the country, better, newer hotels sprang up. Then shooters replaced the old clientele.

There was certainly nothing special about the Mustafa. It sat on the crossroads of what became a barricaded street leading to the Ministry of the Interior. The ambience there was no different from that in any run-down roadhouse found at highway exits across the United States. Typically, on Thursday nights – the start of the Afghan weekend – dozens of addled-looking middle-aged men, mostly in security, could be found drinking heavily at the bar. The prostitutes, Jenner thought, didn't look much different.

On one such night a single gunshot rang out, followed by more rounds from an automatic weapon. One second Jenner was enjoying a double vodka and tonic, the next he was looking at everyone's shoelaces as he crawled on his hands and knees out of the door and on to the street.

When Jenner stood up, he came face to face with Randall Benjamin Hart. Balding, mid-forties, a good Southern Baptist, 'Jungle Ben' had grown up in Tehran, the Farsi-speaking son of an American soldier and now himself a three-star general.

Jenner and Jungle Ben had first met stateside at West Point, the military academy, a long time ago when they were young cadets training to be officers. Later, they'd served together, when both had thoughts of derring-do. Once good friends, their lives had taken very different paths.

Jenner had come to actively dislike the way the Service had changed into a good ole boys' network, and after five years he resigned his commission in disgust. The men hadn't seen each other until they reconnected in the Kabul jungle.

Hart, for his part, counted the American ambassador and the head of ISAF as personal friends. His role was ambiguous, but Jenner knew he had access and money, and with his easy fluency in Dari was a prized asset.

In those early days, with the friendship rekindled, the two men made their way around town. Over the next few weeks they drank at the biker bar where a Confederate flag hung proudly over a pool table and 1970s American rock 'n' roll played. They hung out at the Elbow Room, a posh bar which almost made you believe you were in a glamorous establishment in the Bay Area. Shooter bars served beer from kegs, had darts tournaments, and there was inevitably a fight on the hour, while at tree-hugger bars intellectuals argued politics. They went to all of them.

Jenner told Hart that he had been hired to work for an American company that converted forty-foot containers into latrines and living spaces for the US government. The opportunity had come at the perfect time. He had grown tired of living in Manila, where he had been based for the last fifteen years. His long-time girlfriend had woken up one morning and simply dumped him. She had literally turned to him in bed and told him to get out. He was restless and broke. But it wasn't the money that lured him to Kabul; it was the sense of adventure.

Summer 2008

Over the following years, Jenner lost the optimism he had arrived with – a typical all-American boy who had come to help rebuild a broken country. Hart was much less sensitive and much more fiercely ambitious. He was interested more in his own future than in that of Afghanistan. So when Hart invited his old friend for dinner, Jenner thought something might be up.

Hart ate at the Taverna, one of his favourite restaurants, not only for its fine Lebanese food, but also because it served red wine in teapots. As he was on active duty, drinking was forbidden, but maverick that he was, Hart broke this rule like so many others.

Hart did, as it turned out, need Jenner to do a job for him, and for a fleeting moment Jenner felt almost hopeful again. The contract was to arm an 800-man private security detail whose mission was to guard a mere fourteen American soldiers while they mentored the Afghan Security Forces. The men needed weapons – either M16s or AK-47s.

Due to various political, economic and logistical restraints, the US Army no longer guarded itself, instead outsourcing security to American corporations like Demonix. The reason they decided on 800 security guards,

Jenner supposed, was because some jackass was hell-bent on 'winning hearts and minds' in this remote part of western Afghanistan. That meant engaging with the locals in the nearby village in an area known to be a hotbed of Taliban insurgency, and a black hole where criminal gangs hijacked NATO supply trucks.

But nothing could ever have prepared Jenner for the Kafkaesque goings-on and the insanity and stupidity of it all. It was a typical Catch-22 situation, the only possible explanation being that there were quotas to fill and a budget worth billions of dollars that had to be spent within a certain timeframe. It didn't seem to matter if the job got done or even where the money went.

It was, thought Jenner cynically, the usual clusterfuck. Keen to award the contract, the US Army refused to supply any provisions for the contractor, lest the deal come back to bite them. In particular they would not provide a Common Access Card (CAC). Without this active-duty US personnel ID card, there was no way to get on the heavily fortified American base. It was the golden key. And without getting on the base there was no way to deliver the contract. Had the government given Jenner a letter of arming authorization, he could have bought the necessary weapons in the States and had them shipped via military air. By sheer good fortune, but mostly by military incompetence, Jenner had been able to hold on to his CAC.

The forces were disorganized and Jenner hated the way soldiers were rotated out every six to twelve months; it gave them no time to get a handle on the situation and to get to know and understand the personalities and terrain. He reckoned the Allies won World War Two because men stayed in the field and fought. Nowadays, the military used laptops more than rifles.

Even more, Jenner loathed the officers who cared only for promotion, and each rotation saw some new unworkable scheme implemented by men who would not be there to see the results. Jenner was shocked and embarrassed. To be classified as a war there had to be a clearly defined enemy. This was not a war at all, he thought. This was a mess.

As mysterious as Hart's role was, Jenner's own CV never really properly fit together either. His business-development identity was plausible, but everyone just assumed he was a spy. How else could he arrange all these deals? But he had the perfect cover – as an American, the possibilities for Jenner were limitless. In the handful of years he'd lived in Kabul, Jenner went everywhere and knew everyone. He had played and partied in Kabul, gone fishing for native trout in the mountain streams near Kunduz and duck hunting in the swamps and rivers in Jalalabad. He had shot game since he was old enough to drag a .22-calibre rifle into the woods, a skill he knew could come in handy. With a weapon in his hands something inside him clicked; shooting insurgents was no different from shooting fowl in a flooded Mississippi marsh.

Jenner knew there was only one solution. And that was purchasing the weapons on the black market. Hart had approached Jenner to do the job because he knew he could get round the bullshit.

Jenner now needed to find 900 automatic weapons. The best course of action was to start with a trip to Sher-Pur, a district in central Kabul full of gaudy, overbuilt houses, allegedly financed by the profits from narcotics. One of the biggest was the poppy palace of the Walrus, a notorious former warlord who had found a comfortable niche in the modern Afghan establishment. He travelled in a huge convoy, which launched out of his ornate sprawling mansion, with him nestled somewhere inside one of the dozens of vehicles piled high with armed guards. If anyone had access to weapons, it was the Walrus.

It had been Jenner's trusted Afghan sidekick who had arranged a meeting. In the way that things work in Afghanistan, Mahmoud knew somebody who knew somebody who knew somebody who knew the Walrus.

At first, there was the awkward silence, but the Walrus gave Jenner a lot of respect. After all, he had once been America's man in Afghanistan. Servants came in with tea, and Jenner practically fell asleep through all the formalities that went on for close to an hour: 'I am sincerely honoured by your presence and how your country is helping us . . . I wish you and your family great peace and prosperity for the future . . . God bless all of your endeavours and I hope this meeting will be a sign of peace for the future and that we may establish a long and lasting, trustworthy bond . . .' The translator's monotone voice grated on Jenner's nerves, making for a deadly combination with the doors and windows which were kept shut to keep out the dirt and dust.

Tea finally made way for the Johnnie Walker Black Label Jenner had brought with him. Jenner and the Walrus reclined on the long, flat, hard cushions covered in carpet material and placed around the periphery of the room. The gilt furniture stood in the centre and was used only for foreign dignitaries. The staff placed the bottle in the middle of a very valuable silk Afghan rug, hand-loomed by small children and women.

The Walrus liked to drink, usually to excess. Jenner had learned to hold his liquor, although admittedly it wasn't always obvious. The two men downed the bottle straight, and Jenner listened to the Walrus's deep, bellowing voice as he boasted of grisly Soviet exploits.

Jenner needed guns, and any negotiation was going to be tricky. A request to purchase arms was prohibited by Afghan law – any direct mention and the ex-warlord might have thought Jenner was CIA or CNN trying to entrap him. But with the bottle finished, it felt safe enough to make an initial move.

Jenner trod gingerly. He began with the observation that when he had been in the former mujahideen's home base, Mazar-e Sharif, he had seen a few containers at an Afghan government building filled with rusty and broken Kalashnikovs. These guns, he said, could be cleaned up and refurbished. 'Sir, I am sure you know that,' Jenner continued, not wanting the ex-warlord to feel he was treating him like an idiot.

The Walrus grunted something in Dari, which the nervous boy translated: 'Interesting. Continue.' The monotone was really annoying Jenner now.

'Have you thought of what happens should these fall into the hands of the Taliban?' Jenner was pretty sure the

Walrus had considered this. After all, the Walrus was an extremely experienced fighter. 'I would be happy to remove them for you,' he concluded.

The Walrus sat motionless, as if he had heard nothing. There was no acknowledgement, but Jenner knew the seed had been planted. They polished off another bottle, and then Jenner bade the ex-warlord goodnight. He thought of embracing the burly fighter, kissing him on both cheeks, then reconsidered, and instead put his hand over his heart, mumbled *khoda hafiz*, and left.

One of the effeminate attendants, sheepish in his mannerisms in contrast to the powerful impact of his boss, indicated that supplying Jenner with modern and working automatic weapons was something he could do. Kohl rimmed his half-closed dark eyes, and he wore a typical multi-coloured embroidered silk cap above his wide, broad Uzbek face.

This way the Walrus kept his hands clean, and his followers scooped up healthy commissions. Jenner's assistant attended to the details, making it clear that he would pay no more than US$375 apiece and that the weapons had to be in good working order. Needless to say, it would be a cash deal – no receipts, no records – and no taxes for the IRS.

Jenner and his trusted ADC drove away from the Walrus's mansion feeling satisfied. Jenner drank a beer and smoked a cigarette on the way back to their very own container that night. Checkpoints had started to pop up around the city, but this was still before the 'Ring of Steel' was official policy. At 3 a.m. the streets were eerily quiet. The stop on Qala-e Fatullah Road didn't even seem manned until a sleepy Afghan National Police guard appeared. After a few exchanges, the leather-faced man reached into the car, lifted Jenner's brewski from his lap and downed a big gulp. He then reached in a second time and removed Jenner's cigarette; he put it to his lips and inhaled, taking one very long, very deep drag. Keeping the beer and smoke, the very stoned guard said '*Buru*,' with a big smile on his face. Jenner drove away, as instructed.

In preparation for the deal, Jenner arranged to meet the manager of the only foreign bank in town, and this, he hoped, would be the start of a beautiful friendship. As everything in the country was paid for in cash – from houses to expensive weddings – a request for half a million US dollars was not out of the ordinary.

Earlier that day, Jenner had purchased three green knock-off Adidas holdalls at Roshan Plaza Mall in the centre of town for $10 each. He'd arranged with the bank manager for two of the bags to be stuffed with scrap paper from the photocopy machine, so they looked about three-quarters full of dirty laundry. Jenner laughed at his own pun. The one with the money had a single paperclip twisted around the zipper.

This was Jenner's rule of thumb: a bundle of US$10K in $100 bills was about the usual size of a ladies' wallet. Ten of those fit easily into a briefcase, and half a million greenbacks would fit into a small gym bag.

That night Jenner used the money as a pillow, finding it surprisingly uncomfortable.

Psyched and prepped, Jenner began the task in earnest; he knew that once the suppliers saw his face, he would be marked for future harassment, might even be a kidnap target, although they usually preferred Afghan businessmen whose families paid ransoms. If anything went wrong, no government would pay for his release. And Hart, too, would deny all knowledge of the deal. Jenner also knew that if he didn't provide the weapons he would have defaulted on his contract, and would most likely be blacklisted. But that was the least of his worries. If the Afghan government caught him, he could be deported, jailed and possibly murdered.

The plan was to make the swap – guns for money – in broad daylight. Once the weapons were checked and loaded into the van, they would be airlifted to Kandahar, the Taliban stronghold in the south. After the transaction Jenner would need to be out of the country for at least two months to let things cool down. If he stayed, the dealers would likely pressure him to make another deal. Or they might change their minds and demand more money, even though the business was concluded. His main worry was that they might bump him off and keep both the money and the guns.

Along with Mahmoud, Jenner worked with two Americans. Cruz was Puerto Rican and everyone called him JLo (his parents came from the same town as Jennifer Lopez's), which made him turn red with rage. Joe hailed from the Lone Star State, and he just talked and talked and talked – even by Texan standards. Both men had huge egos, little experience and not too many brain cells – and neither could think of anything better than to watch Jenner fail. They were also competitive.

That day, Cruz's job was to drive the Toyota Surf from the compound to the meeting point. As a de-miner, Cruz had nerves of steel. And boy, would he need them, Jenner thought. Cruz would also take the two Afghan PSDs, as well as the Nepalese guard, while Jenner drove the van with Mahmoud for company.

Joe worked inside Bagram airfield, the main American military base, eleven kilometres south-east of the capital and the size of a small city. There was no need for Jenner to tell him about the real deal. He explained he was doing a job for the army, and had to leave the van with him.

As the appointed time grew close, Mahmoud called the three Afghan suppliers, and gave them an ETA outside Bagram. As there were only two roads, the vendors would know the route Jenner and his men were going to take. No doubt they had people staked out along both.

Three barely functioning Toyota estate cars that looked like typical Afghan taxis pulled up at the rendezvous point. As the deal needed to go down fast, the men backed the cars into a circle. The group was parked in the empty dirt lot in full view of the mounted machine-gun posts that protected the base. Even the Afghans, whose territory it was, would not have taken the risk of whacking Jenner right under the noses of all that US military might, especially if they thought he was on active duty.

Each supplier, accompanied by a guard, had done his best to dress like a legitimate businessman, wearing typical Pakistani 'manjammies', piran tomban and plastic sandals on feet grey from dry skin.

There were no formalities – highly unusual in a highly

formal and extremely polite society. The Afghans were well behaved, thought Jenner, and did not interfere as the weapons were transferred, waiting quietly off to one side until it was done.

Jenner had devised a system. As all the guns came in rice sacks, he would unload one at a time. He would take each weapon out, 'clear' it to make sure it wasn't loaded, dry fire it to make sure at least the basic parts were operational, then hand it first to one guard to remove the stock, then on to another to inventory it. Cruz would then place each gun in a Gorilla box – a large black plastic container used by the military for shipping – and, lastly, Mahmoud would close it.

The system worked well. It was early morning and the Americans on the base were too busy listening to their iPods to take much notice of the transaction; Jenner and his crew just got lucky. In less than ninety minutes they had packed 913 Kalashnikovs into twenty-seven Gorilla boxes stacked in the van. Only two AKs were in questionable condition.

As the loading was finishing, Jenner called out, 'All done?' When he heard the answer, 'Yes', he walked round and closed the doors, which had remained open throughout the operation. He slipped into the driver's seat and shut his door gently without making a sound. As he turned the ignition, the group looked up, puzzled, but not particularly alarmed. Then Jenner put his foot down and drove as fast as he could for 1,000 metres, directly into the base, dust flying everywhere, on to American territory.

Inside the base Jenner drove to the Traffic Management Office run by Kellogg Brown & Root, huge American contractors. He said he had firearms and ammunition ready to transport to KAF. He showed them the authorization letter for military transport and the contract number.

After two hours of paperwork, Jenner took the weapons and ammo inside the flight line where KBR staff helped him 'palletize' the shipment to be loaded on to the C-130 military aircraft. He arranged to escort the cargo as the official 'pallet rider'.

Next, he called Cruz, who was still waiting in the dust with the men and told him to take everyone back to the compound.

'Roger, dodger,' said Cruz. Irritated, Jenner told him he would not be returning.

Mahmoud then gave the duffel bag with the paperclip to Hamid, the Walrus's man, who would divide the spoils.

That done, Jenner had twelve hours to kill before the plane took off. He went to the PX, where he stocked up on supplies, then grabbed a cheeseburger and mega-large Coke at Burger King.

Later that evening, the gunmetal grey Hercules C-130, its windows blacked out as usual for a night flight, landed at KAF. The giant plane disgorged its men and cargo from the rear, putting Jenner in mind of a roaring lion, its mouth open to devour its prey.

Jenner descended, desperate to pee having refused to use the barrel just behind the cockpit. Not that anyone was interested in watching, but all the same there were four long benches of soldiers strapped in behind him.

By the time he came out a few minutes later the pallets had disappeared, sent far and wide to various locations. He couldn't believe it and walked over to the office to get some answers. The right hand didn't seem to know what the left hand was doing, he discovered. He was angry, tired and frustrated. How, he thought to himself, was it possible to lose 913 automatic rifles?

It took Jenner all night to find the guns, but when he did, he thought it might be the happiest moment of his life.

Spring 2011

I never did find out what Jenner did with my RPGs. I guess I should have asked.

be Kandahar before heading north to Mazar. A teeny little bit alarming, but also quite interesting because, as every Canadian knows, there is a Tim Hortons on the KAF boardwalk. The question asked by any non-Canadian (at least, those who have never been to Kandahar Air Field) is who or what is a Tim Hortons.

Tim Horton was a famous Canadian hockey player who started a doughnut and coffee shop that soon became a nationwide chain and then an institution, and in 2006 the company opened a replica for the troops. So while Canadians might be fighting their bloodiest battles since Korea in the 1950s, in this insurgent heartland Tim Hortons rules. It had become a rite of passage for any self-respecting Canadian journalist to head straight there.

KAF was the size of a small prairie town, and boasted the busiest single runway in the world. Despite my appalling sense of direction, I began walking down the dusty road to Tim Hortons with utterly fierce determination. The Taliban had no idea what they were up against.

I question where my devotion to Tim Hortons comes from, and assume it is sentimental, something that links me to home, although I am hardly a refugee and voluntarily chose to leave Toronto and move to London. Their filter coffee is much milder than Starbucks' burnt brew, but not watery, and the little round Timbits line up in the box like small, happy, bite-size faces of delicious sour cream and chocolate-glazed doughnut holes, staring up and smiling, saying EAT ME.

There is something surreal about being in the most foreign of places and experiencing a totally parallel universe. I understand the rationale of having aspects of home in a hostile environment. Stranger still, perhaps, to think that people worked at KAF – from Canada and other countries – and never ventured beyond the wire during their entire six-month tour.

I bought a box of Timbits to share with two aid workers I had met on the flight. Rather than my usual hot filter coffee, I opted for an iced cappuccino frappé. A moment of sheer, inexplicable Kandahari madness.

Mission accomplished, I had to find my way back or I would miss the plane. The pilot had threatened he wouldn't wait and would leave me in Kandahar. I could think of worse things. There were always stories to uncover – stories that helped me understand the different players in the alien landscape I was trying to interpret as a journalist. Even breathing the air in Kandahar gave me a new perspective. And KAF was another slice of a unique Afghan life that would at some point pass into history and later oblivion.

I started walking back in the intense heat, wandering and poking around, strolling down the streets until a car stopped and the military driver asked to see some identification. He was horrified to discover that a journalist had been let loose without authority on the base (of course, that had crossed my mind too), and rather than let me roam, he drove me directly back to the landing strip, where the flight had been delayed another hour because of engine trouble.

Camp Northern Lights

Much has been written about counterinsurgency in Afghanistan, but the real story for me was what I believe could have been a much more effective strategy in this year of the Tipping Point. Perhaps I had spent too much time in the loo, pristine and clean and simply divine. Because at Swedish-run Camp Northern Lights, using soap and water and washing one's hands – an activity that is second nature to most of us – is only the beginning of a procedure so detailed, so complex, so sublime, it was a campaign that had to be carried out with military precision. I was completely captivated.

Cleaning starts when you open the door onto a fairly standard facility suffused with the dull lighting of public utilities. You enter the cubicle and find the written

81

instructions tacked to the door. Antibacterial fluid is left on the floor of each stall, and is to be used on the handle of the loo, on the seat and on the lock and handle of the door. A mission in itself.

Next step: washing your hands – an equally intricate performance that makes surgeons scrubbing up for theatre look unhygienic. According to the instructions, you must first wash your hands with soap for about thirty-five seconds, using your elbow to turn off the tap. Then, you have to dry your hands under the thermonuclear-powered hand dryer. When they are dry, you use the hand sanitizer – one of the twentieth century's greatest inventions – and take a brown paper towel to wipe your hands. You then use said brown paper towel to open the door.

The process begins again when you walk across to the mess hall, where you must repeat decontamination procedures before being allowed access to the excellent fresh salmon. In fact, what becomes apparent is that you are so busy killing germs you forget about killing the enemy.

Being a Swedish base, there was a sauna. (A Swede must have a sauna like a Canadian must have a doughnut.) And after the (single-sex) sauna, there was the power shower.

I can't remember the rules of washing in the shower – the instructions that had to be followed to ensure germ

warfare went down the plughole and not out on a date –
but the sheer force of the water and the very nature of its
Swedish luxury would surely win over even Mullah Omar.
Forget the COIN strategy – what the insurgents needed to be
brought on side was power showers.

Camp Northern Lights was situated near Balkh,
once a major world city, sacked in 1220 by Genghis Khan.
Zoroaster is believed to be buried there and the famous poet
Rūmī was born and educated there in the thirteenth century.
It was also known as the kingdom of Bactra, and is located
about twenty kilometres from Mazar-e Sharif, which became
the regional capital in the 1870s. It seemed crazy not to visit
both cities.

At the centre of Mazar is a sublimely exquisite blue-
tiled mosque, believed by Afghans alone to be the site of
the tomb of Ali ibn Abi Talib, cousin and son-in-law of
the Prophet Muhammad. The shrine is magnificent and
peaceful, each tile intricately designed and the turquoise rich
and outstanding.

Ted was in his US Army uniform as we walked along
a path lined with fake palm trees to the forecourt of the
mosque. We weren't permitted to go any further.

White pigeons live in the courtyard and locals believe
that every seventh one is a spirit. To our right, women in

white burqas seemed to float by, carried along by the slight breeze. Three of these white apparitions, all with painted red toenails, drifted in our direction. A small boy accompanied them, holding a rose in his hand – a real one, not the popular plastic variety; urged on by his mother, he handed it shyly to Ted. We were stunned. Ted took the boy's hand and moved it in my direction. I took the rose, and said, '*Tashakor*' – 'Thank you' – in Dari about a million times. As alien as this country sometimes seems, and as distant as it is in so many ways, this small human gesture confirmed what I have always believed: that fundamentally, we are all the same. These are all the little pieces in between.

I don't know if the women smiled or not. I certainly did, and I took the full, fat flower back with me and pressed it between the graph-paper pages of my field notebook. It remains there today – squashed, withered and brown with that little fleck of red that so dramatically contrasted with the women's white outfits, but matched their toenails. And, like so many things from Afghanistan, it remains in my heart.

The next day Sakhi came to take me to Balkh. Sakhi was an interesting young man who worked as a translator. We went back to the mosque and Sakhi arranged for me to go to the library to look at the collection of Korans there. We walked around barefoot, me tiptoeing as I had forgotten to wear socks. Something about the empty space calmed me, even though I'm not remotely religious.

Following an afternoon sightseeing and chatting, Sakhi invited me back to his house for tea. He had talked about his two-year-old daughter, by whom he was completely enthralled. I asked him what he wanted her to be when she grew up. 'I don't mind,' he said (a bit put out, I sensed). 'I want her to decide. She can be a doctor or a lawyer or whatever, but it is her choice.'

That seemed like a remarkably liberal attitude, but then the north is more tolerant than the Sunni south. He told me about his wife, a cousin who came from a neighbouring province. She had left school in grade five and married him when she was very young. Her life was dedicated to looking after Leda, their daughter, who had a fabulous and very lively personality. Like her father, I too fell in love with her.

As shy and timid as her mother was, Leda was an extroverted little girl who wanted to show me all her toys and jewellery. She reminded me of my niece, who wasn't much older. She immediately spotted the enamelled bracelet I had been given by one of the merchants from Chicken Street and put it on her arm, proudly displaying it, so there was really nothing else for me to do but give it to her. This little fireball clearly ruled the roost; who knows – maybe she really will be able to do what she wants when she grows up.

Sakhi's wife had made tea, which he served. She was reluctant to come out, but after much coaxing from her husband, and a bit of insistence from me, she emerged to say hello. She was uncomfortable. Her life revolved around her family in their compound. She was painfully shy and I felt bad having forced her to socialize. She couldn't have stayed for more than a couple of minutes before leaving, palpably relieved.

Back at Camp Northern Lights I shared my capsule-like room with a Swedish aid worker for one night. Even in this bug-free zone she slept under her zip-up mosquito net tent – something I coveted. She wore white socks and sandals, which poked out from under her long, wide skirt, fitting every stereotype I could conjure up. There was a sense of sadness about her, but perhaps that was simply my own projection. We didn't speak a word to each other, despite sleeping less than a metre apart, and in the morning she was gone. I never found out who she was or even her name.

Meandering back to my room the second night I stumbled upon the bar and went in with the intention of saying a quick goodnight to Ted. Instead, I got caught in conversation. A Swede soon rolled in; his name was Peter.

'Did you ever read the Heidi books?' I asked him.

'No,' he responded, surprised. 'Why do you ask?'

'Peter is the name of the Swiss goatherd whom Heidi befriends,' I replied. 'She marries him in the sequel.'

'So, am I your destiny?' he asked.

A pretty cool line, I thought. Turned out he wasn't, but he did take me to the Swedish church nearby, which looked like something out of a Strindberg play. It would not have surprised me if I'd walked out of there into the bleak Scandinavian winter. Instead, it was a cold night in May under the bright stars of an Afghan sky.

The next day Peter was off to Kabul. And I had more lessons to learn.

7. Lessons on Drinking Water from a Bottle

I hardly notice him at La Cantina, standing by the wall. Most Thursday nights this Tex-Mex restaurant is heaving. Soldiers don't tend to come here, and if they do, they certainly don't wear their uniforms, so Nathaniel looks out of place. Kabul in early 2007 is still full of foreigners trying to put the situation right. He is a man sent by God (and government), his mission clear. His fundamentalist Christian faith is spookily similar to the conservative mantra of the true believers of Islam. He is like a missionary, with his Christian zeal – here to do God's work.

I walk past the pool table and check him out on the way to the bar, noticing how his full beard almost obscures his fine features. A mutual friend has agreed to meet Nathaniel because he wants a night out in Kabul and doesn't know many people. She takes me along, although I am uninterested in engaging in more idle chit-chat; I've had too much of that – the banter of the bored, the casual, the quick fix, the one-night stand.

The music blares out. People order margaritas and nachos, play pool and mill around. Everyone is looking for something or someone – and that includes Nathaniel. But before my friend catches his eye, she tells me he is married and has three children back in Australia. 'Don't be fooled,' she warns.

A few days later, lured by the promise of a wild party and dinner, neither of which materialize, I visit Nathaniel at his compound on the Jalalabad road. In his little room, tiny and contained, we end up talking and talking. There is a sofa and a desk, a kitchenette, a small bathroom and a bedroom. It's temporary lodging before he moves closer into town. Through a crack in the door I see a photo of his wholesome spouse with their brood of children – Joshua, Luke, Caleb, Ruth: four, not three. It shouldn't have surprised me to learn that his wife sewed her own clothes, cooked and cleaned, looked after the children and milked the cows on their farm.

In the shadow of his real life, locked behind closed doors, he asks to hold my hand, and I say 'No.' I know where that kind of behaviour leads. It is a slippery slope, I tell him. It would lead to where it inevitably does – back into the marriage fold on the farm in the southern hemisphere with a saintly, forgiving, homespun wife: the wife with whom he planted the placenta of each of their four children under

89

different trees. Way too earthy for me. When these Afghan days come to an end, when it is time to go, when the context changes, when the roles are reversed, the home, the wife, the family, the farm, the children, the relatives, the country, the career – all that will win. There is no contest, no matter how wonderful, how easy, how perfect the fit. It is not rocket science.

As Nathaniel's driver takes me on the long, potentially treacherous journey to my home in Qala-e Fatullah, we touch on the situation in Israel and Palestine, as remote a problem as can be imagined in this country with enough difficulties of its own. It's a discussion I am not prepared to have, however, and, as deftly as I can, I switch the conversation to the state of women in Afghanistan. It's easier to deal with.

Waheed, the driver, strikes me as a sensitive, smart guy. His father used to work for the UN, and if the circumstances weren't so volatile, the economy so rife with corruption and the country so broken, I'm sure he would have a fine future in whatever it was he decided to do. I like him. When he takes me home that first night, he complains about Nathaniel because he makes him work long hours. Nathaniel would brush this aside, no doubt annoyed. 'Just do it,' I could hear him say. I soon learn that he irritates a lot of people with his brusque style and lack of professional sensitivity.

Weeks later, in April, a dinner has been arranged at my house, but the American who runs the show has asked that Nathaniel does not attend, believing him to be a security contractor rather than a Rhodes scholar. So we make our own plans to go out.

Nathaniel picks me up wearing camouflage. He has shaved off his beard and is quite spectacularly handsome – fair, with blue eyes and the body of a god. I had no idea. He strikes me, oddly, like F. Scott Fitzgerald's Jay Gatsby, who sprang out of nowhere and arrived fully formed. Unlike Gatsby, Nathaniel would absolutely reject any form of ostentatious wealth, and I cannot imagine he ever killed a man, but perhaps something reminded me of Gatsby's doomed romance with Daisy.

My American housemate is now keen for Nathaniel to stay. The other guests include a top US Administration official who believes in his mission to do good, if not spread democracy in Afghanistan. It's a naivety that the British guests cannot help but deride. Another American guest is leading the fight against poppy cultivation in the south. He has experience, if not answers, having dealt with the FARC and drugs in Colombia. His various exploits were used as the basis for a Hollywood film. Journalist Jon Lee Anderson from the *New Yorker* is there too.

Nathaniel knows them all from work; his is a political mission mandated to lay the foundations for peace. The men talk about the fact that eradicating the poppy crop is not working – the harvest is up 60 per cent this year alone and 2007, it turns out, will be the bumper year for poppy cultivation, reaching a peak of 193,000 hectares. It's the year of opium and the end of optimism. The Americans want to spray the fields with herbicide to eradicate the plant, but the British want to work on alternative livelihoods. It's an industry. Kids take time off school to work in the fields, provincial governors get good commissions and it provides many families with an income; but heroin addiction is also growing in Afghanistan, cheap and available as the drug is. The Taliban takes its cut, too, and either way heroin consumption grows. One British diplomat told me that it was important to get the message over to the Afghans that opium was bad and addictive. It's not so easy to suggest to someone who is in unbearable pain that they should just wait a couple of years until a road is built to the village and a local pharmacy opens that stocks aspirin.

Poppy, politics and Pakistan: these are the key issues that will determine the success of the country – or defeat it. And corruption.

Before we head off I have to say goodnight to the dogs

that live at the compound, Poppy and Hilly, as they have me wrapped around their little paws. I am a willing victim; I believe in winning their affection by constantly providing them with treats. I also allow them to roam around inside and sleep in my room. One of the heads of the PR team had built a doghouse (right under my window) and used to lock them in at night, which they hated. As I thought it was a cruel and stupid thing to do, and I couldn't bear the tormenting sounds of their whimpering, inevitably every night the same pantomime would play out. The rise of their crescendo would catapult me out of bed and I would go downstairs, unlock the doghouse doors and the dogs would bound up to my room to sleep.

I have a particularly close relationship with Hilly, since Poppy is neurotic, jealous, skittish, clearly troubled and in need of some dog therapy. Hilly was rescued from Poppy's jaws hours after she arrived at the house. Poppy had, unprovoked, grabbed Hilly between her teeth and started shaking the smaller dog, which was howling in fear and pain. Somehow the few of us who were there got Poppy to unclamp her jaws and release the wounded puppy, and I scooped Hilly up and cuddled her as she recovered. But Poppy was, of course, part of the sisterhood, canine or otherwise, and we girls stick together.

Nathaniel and I get into the armoured car. The doors are impossibly heavy, and I can barely shut mine. Waheed is at the wheel.

We go to Red Hot 'n' Sizzlin, a restaurant with a big chilli hanging in the front, secured behind barricades, as everything is. It is a funny place, frequented it seems by 'shooters', close protection men and army types when they are either allowed out (not very often) or when they sneak out (occasionally). Americans are pretty much pinned down to their bases. Men crave women's company in this environment and it's easy to get sucked in, which is why they say the odds are good, but the goods are odd.

The conversation does not flow so easily at the beginning. It feels awkward. One part of me resists; I want no emotional or sexual interaction with a married man, not in Afghanistan, war zone or not. I'm not made of steel. And I don't want to fall into the trap of thinking that somehow this will be different.

I haven't seen Nathaniel for weeks, as he's been out of the country on a mission, but today is the day after my birthday, and not only has he remembered, he also has a present for me. It is a lapis lazuli necklace – lots of tiny ropes of the delicate blue beads which are so popular in Afghanistan. Something I haven't yet got round to buying.

94

Something I have been meaning to buy as a souvenir of my time in country. He gives it to me in a little box inlaid with lapis and silver filigree detail. I think that's when the shift happens.

When we get back to my house that night, he comes upstairs. In the doorway he strokes my hair and takes my hand. And then he kisses me, his blue eyes open and staring at me the whole time.

That is as far as things go, as I need to protect myself from him and the chemistry. We fall asleep in each other's arms on the sofa in the sitting room. Poppy and Hilly are there too, part of this new, extended family – Poppy curled up on the floor and Hilly snuggled at my feet.

From then on I see him all the time and speak to him a few times a day. He sucks me in with his inclusiveness, and we become closer and closer, merging together, but this intertwining is the very thing I wanted to avoid. He is always trying to involve me: whether it's an invitation to a party, arranging an interview or calling to see how things are going – these are as seductive and appealing to me as his intellect and physical attractiveness, and I know resistance is ultimately futile. We go everywhere together and it's intoxicating, while he tunnels deeper and deeper into my soul and wraps his heart around mine. He has touched something in me that I cannot fight despite the intellectual rationalization and the realization that only heartbreak lies at the end of the affair.

One night he asks me to meet him at his office after work when the compound is empty, and everyone has gone home. He has already bought me a large map of Afghanistan, and a similar one hangs on his wall. On his wooden desk is an ISAF mug with the campaign logo 'Enduring Freedom' on it. He is dressed in his usual camouflage, the top few buttons of his shirt open.

This is it. The build-up has been intense: weeks of waiting, of wondering, of going back and forth, and then simply the inevitability of it. The intellectual has given way to the emotional and the primeval. Love does extraordinary things. In our own small paradise where time is limited and the end is clear, it doesn't matter that he has such strong faith and I am a true non-believer. Lots of important things don't matter, including what follows – the really, really bad sex.

Our next official outing is the Anzac Day service on 25 April to commemorate the ill-fated World War One campaign at Gallipoli in 1915. Nathaniel picks me up at 5 a.m. with his boss, and we drive to the ISAF HQ.

After the service, I see Nathaniel talking to Dan McNeill, the American four-star general who is head of the NATO-led ISAF mission. I want to interview McNeill. I have already tried the official channels, which have been ineffective, so I seize my opportunity and abruptly, with an uncharacteristic lack of charm, cut short my conversation with Nathaniel's boss and head directly over to them. Nathaniel immediately brings me into the conversation and introduces me. At the appropriate time I ask McNeill for an interview, and he agrees. I am to set it up with his ADC for June as instructed. Nathaniel, as always, is supportive and it's in no small part thanks to him that this happens. It turns out to be a fantastically successful interview – one that is supposed to last for thirty minutes but which goes on for an hour.

Each new general has his own formula to bring the conflict to an end, and McNeill's reputation is that of a war-fighter. 'Stack 'em up like cordwood,' McNeill is reputed to have said about killing the Taliban when he first took over. A Vietnam vet with a grey buzz cut, he had no doubt stacked up a few of the enemy himself. General McNeill, who referred to himself as a 'hard dude', had a line of videos on his shelf. Apparently they could be bought in the local markets. When I asked what they were he gave me a pretty graphic description of what happens when someone is beheaded. He explained how the blood squirts halfway across the room. He said that the barbarous act was rarely a quick guillotine-like execution, but instead one where the victims' necks were slowly hacked through. It did not bear thinking about.

Everyone seemed to have a theory for how to swing the war and eliminate the Taliban. Armchair generals were quick to criticize, but didn't actually have any magic solutions themselves, which irritated McNeill. If it was so easy, as everyone kept telling him, then why didn't they just come and do it themselves? He had a point. General McNeill asked me some tough tactical questions – like what would I do to win the war? He said if I answered correctly I could have his job. Actually, I asked if I could have his job if I answered correctly. And those blue eyes crinkled up with laughter.

Of course, I was under no illusion. I didn't have a clue. If the top military minds in the US and UK armies couldn't sort Afghanistan out, what answers could I seriously provide? But power showers and Tim Hortons would make a promising start, I thought.

•••

In May, Nathaniel arranges for us to go to Bamiyan, and gets us on the UN flight manifest. I have arranged to interview the female governor.

The night before the trip we stay at the UN guesthouse, UNOCA, in Kabul. When you come face to face with the organization the scale is dumbfounding. Here, at this sprawling compound with a pool and gardens, UN staffers hang out, pass through, eat, drink, meet and work.

In Afghanistan there are many reasons to drink bottled water, not least the altitude, which dehydrates you, and to flush the dust and other dirt from your system. There is always water to hand. At the American bases there are thousands upon thousands of crate-loads of small bottles everywhere, and here too at the UN compound. Glasses seem an unnecessary formality, and so we drink from the bottle.

Drinking water from a bottle causes all sorts of problems. Small droplets fall from my lips. It's provocative, though unintentionally so; more like straightforward incompetence. Nathaniel sits on the edge of the bed. 'Shall I show you how to drink water from a bottle?' It is my first lesson. Taking a large plastic container of Healthy Life, he puts it to his mouth, wrapping both perfectly formed lips around it. 'See?' he says. One gulp. Two. Three. 'See,' he says again. 'If you do it, make sure that no oxygen gets out.'

He puts the bottle down and continues his demonstration. Perfect, controlled, excellently executed, just like him. 'Now you try,' he says. He makes me practise, small sips – odd how I find it so difficult.

In the early morning we head to the airport. Spring has revealed a new Kabul. The seven-year drought is over, and the Kabul River is no longer a trickle; instead, it is about to burst its banks. However, the roads remain as heavily pockmarked as in winter and this makes it impossible for anyone to drive in a straight line. Sometimes driving feels like a game of chicken where everyone is heading down the centre, no one moving until the last second. Nobody has a legitimate driving licence – most have bought one on the black market, usually from a corrupt Department of Transport official.

We drive past one of my favourite shops, which sells rolls of green turf. At some of the traffic roundabouts, battered white-and-red-striped metal umbrellas stand tall above the zigzagging lines of cars, which belch out black fumes; traffic cops sit on raised stands underneath them, talking on the telephone, talking to each other and often talking to drivers who pass by – friends or acquaintances, always men. I love these scenes and take lots of pictures, with their good-natured approval.

Afghanistan is visually sumptuous, and my eyes soak in everything. When you say to an Afghan that something is beautiful, they say your eyes are beautiful. The street merchants stock a variety of colourful goods. One sells a spherical white cheese they spray with water. Donkeys relax by the side of the road, eating. Men and boys sleep in their wagons, some waiting for business.

Our helicopter to Bamiyan stops off at Nili, the capital of Daikundi province, slap-bang in the middle of the country. From the air, the landscape is desolate and beautiful; there are mud and rocks and patches of green with trees. On the ground, large, round, handmade flat cakes of animal dung bake in the sun, and a muddy river snakes through the mountain terrain. In the late spring the last bits of snow cling to the mountainside.

Little girls trundle to school with their white hijabs wrapped around their heads, the ubiquitous fake flowers attached to the sides. They look wonderful and cheerful. In the Hazarajat region women are visible, and it is peaceful. Or rather, seemingly peaceful.

Other Heidi is also on our UN flight. She works for an American company that provides funding and training for the police. She is here to sort out problems, as an international team will be coming to assess them in a few weeks' time.

101

The difficulties start with the fact that nobody can find the police chief, so the deputy is rustled up instead. We are ushered into his office, which is dominated by three pictures of President Karzai. A man brings in the obligatory green Afghan tea and boiled sweets. The deputy police chief is handsome in a way, with a black moustache and a forthright and serious manner.

One of the upcoming tests will be to see if the recruits can read or write. But the recruits have more pressing problems, the deputy police chief explains. 'Night letters' have been dropped at some of their homes. These are the preliminary terror tactics used by the Taliban to stop locals working with foreigners or foreign-funded projects, like this one. The progression of intimidation culminates with beheading.

The meeting lasts about forty minutes, and when it is over we take a short walk down to the river, just to have a quick glance at the landscape before we catch the helicopter, waiting outside, and head to Bamiyan.

The valley in Bamiyan is verdant, spiritual, tranquil, calm and unspoiled. Nathaniel thinks it is no accident that this site was revered by the ancient Buddhists. In complete contrast to chaotic Kabul, Bamiyan is a neat, ordered little town with five hotels, one run by a Japanese woman and her Afghan husband. She cooks Japanese food. How extraordinary. The main artery consists of a few streets on a grid, a town mainly populated by NGOs and charities. Our accommodation is at the UN guesthouse run by a man from Nepal. Photographer Steve McCurry is also there. (He took the iconic shot of the young Afghan girl with the amazing green eyes for the cover of *National Geographic* in 1985.)

I cannot wait for everyone else to go to sleep, so I can finally be with Nathaniel, but the evening and the conversation seem endless. Finally, the lights go off at 11 p.m. The dark is intense and the night cold. Thankfully, this is not one of those times Nathaniel decides to use Vegemite as an aphrodisiac. I am relieved; it's a cultural divide no bridge can cross. Nothing has improved in this area and tonight's antics remind me of some kind of Olympic sport. I'm tossed like a salad and I'm not sure where my limbs are.

In the morning we go to see the remains of the beautiful sandstone buddhas that were carved into a cliff. For over 1,400 years a pair of magnificent statues, the larger fifty-five metres tall, overlooked Bamiyan valley until a Taliban edict declared that these 'non-Islamic' sculptures had to be destroyed. In 2001 they dynamited this extraordinary part of Afghanistan's cultural heritage.

Until a few years ago, about 200 families lived in the rock-hewn caves behind what UNESCO deemed a world heritage site. Pieces of rock from the shattered statues are now stored in a temporary warehouse, where they have been catalogued, and we pay 160Afs each to get in. Through a narrow stone staircase you can climb to the top of the niche in which the larger statue once stood.

From our vantage point we stop to look across the valley. Nathaniel points out Shar-i-Gholghola, the city of sighs. It is the ruins of an ancient town destroyed by the founder of the Mongol empire, Genghis Khan. Ragged children with runny noses clamber about, climbing as naturally up and down the hills as the goats that wander everywhere.

When the Taliban came to this region, they destroyed whatever they could. The ancient shrines in the mountain complex were desecrated, faces and any human representation were gouged out of pictures and shoeprints were left on the ceilings of the shrines. The Talibs left graffiti, but I cannot find Mullah Omar's signature anywhere.

Nathaniel drags me up and down. It is exhilarating and exhausting. Overlooking this staggering valley, our Hazara guide, a Shia, comments that the Taliban, Sunni Pashtuns from the south, didn't only hate women, they hated people. He's right.

That evening we go to the Kiwi PRT for dinner at the Buddha Café. It is a freezing, windy night, but I'm in luck because it also happens to be fish-and-chip night. Also on the menu, quite unbelievably, there truly are fried Mars bars (I cannot believe people actually eat this) and delicious curly fries (which I can believe too easily).

While Nathaniel goes off to do his thing, I talk to the camp padre. It feels like an episode of *M*A*S*H*. The padre tells me a story about a four-year-old girl sold as a child bride because the father couldn't afford to keep her. Somehow an international agency found out and brought her back and she is now in an orphanage. There are endless stories of shocking brutality and cultural clashes – of cruelty, sadness, struggle, hardship and unendurable compromise. It's never-ending.

The next day Nathaniel and I drive up to Lake Band-e Amir, leaving the guesthouse early. It is one of the most magnificent places I have ever seen. This group of lakes, overflowing today with snowmelt, used to be a thriving holiday destination. There are battered swan pedalos, and it costs 100Afs for a ride in the Donald Duck boat. The speedboat seems a safer bet.

The water is an astonishing lapis blue and the place is deserted. Despite what seemed like a better choice of vessel, we get stuck in the middle. The icy water does not feel friendly, should we have to swim back.

Later that afternoon, when we walk through a small stream, the water *is* incredibly cold, numbing my feet, but not quite enough to dull the pain from stepping barefoot on the rocks and pebbles. Nathaniel keeps his boots on and they do not dry for hours. We are hiking, talking, holding hands – hopefully out of sight of any observers. Any physical display of affection between men and women in this country can be fatal.

The only sounds are those of Nathaniel's voice and our feet splashing in the water as we hike. Noiselessly into this still, idyllic scene, dozens and dozens of woolly, fat-bottomed sheep roam down the near-vertical slope of the mountain to drink this fresh, cool water, and I only notice them when I happen to turn round.

Months later, in England, when I walk across an old stone bridge in Arundel, memories of this day will flood back, transporting me to Afghanistan, to a happier time with Nathaniel. On that clear English summer's day, clouds gather on the far edges of the horizon, casting an unearthly light over the East Sussex farmland before the storm comes in. Only there, real swans glide effortlessly by, underneath the bridge – dozens of elegant, white, long-necked birds, with their black-rimmed eyes giving them a slightly mad and menacing air.

We decide to drive back to Kabul, which takes almost ten hours, passing all too quickly with endless conversation. How can two people talk so much? Despite our differences – and there are many on quite a profound level, not least religion – we understand each other and I feel sure of myself in his company. He is also enormously helpful while I am researching my interview with McNeill, impressing on me how key the issue of civilian casualties will become – which it does.

The road is really more like a track in the mud. On a green mountainside the word for Allah is spelled out in white rocks. We stop to look and take pictures, and Nathaniel and I walk down to the river. German journalists died in similar circumstances, having outraged the locals with their open sexuality. Risk is ever-present, often unfelt but there, under the radar, forgotten and ignored. What is it that we have, this passion, I keep asking myself.

At the outskirts of Kabul we stop at a roadside restaurant, which consists of a few ramshackle tables. There is a vat of boulani, which is fried bread stuffed, in this case, with potatoes. Carb on carb. It is as delicious as it is fattening and unhealthy. Nathaniel is much braver than I am and eats everything, including the uncooked greens; he also wipes

107

his hands on the communal towel and uses the bowl of hot sauce that people dip and double-dip into.

A boy comes round selling stuffed toy animals; I want to buy one but decide not to, which is a mistake because it would have given him some money and would have made a fitting present for my niece.

On the road into Kabul we pass the InterContinental Hotel, which has a great view of the city. More interestingly, it has a pool, around which are tables set for a formal dinner with white tablecloths and silver cutlery, and waiters dressed up ready to serve. The wind blows the skirt of the tablecloth. It's too blustery to talk so we go inside.

The lobby has red upholstered armchairs, gilt accents, chandeliers and marble pillars. It is where Nathaniel and I proceed to split up. This game, this parallel life, does not sit well with me, it goes against my nature and my personality, less so for Nathaniel, who is better able to compartmentalize. He cannot let go of his other world. Does it matter? It is only a question of time anyway because we are both leaving. Soon. Very, very soon. Nathaniel has a trip to Pakistan arranged which will give him time to commune with God, to be with nature, and to walk in the hills and think. He will probably ask his god for forgiveness. How he justifies his adultery eludes me, but I don't care to ask.

When he returns he gives me a book he has brought from Chitral, about the tragic life of a woman, and tells me how much I have gotten to him. Something he didn't expect. He needed perspective. He tells me that if we lived in a different world, one where we could be together, he would choose me. Maybe he's lying, but he says that what started as a casual affair, something that ticked to a countdown, unexpectedly turned into something real.

We get back together again, but time is running out. In the giant hourglass I can see each grain of sand falling, heralding the end.

I am trying to remember what made me agree to have a joint going-away party on this, the last night. Another mistake. I cannot speak, while he parties on, talking away. I have to go upstairs because I cannot function. I am too sad. I assume he will follow, but hours seem to pass before the door opens and this alcohol-infused, rather jolly person looks in to see what's happening. How can he not want to spend every last second with me, to have these final hours imprinted on his mind, his soul and in his heart? Instead, he chooses to be with the people with whom he has worked for the last six months. He promises to come up soon, but again I wait static and comatose. I wait for the end. Like an execution.

Once again, the end does not turn out as I imagine. He gets into bed, picks up the bible that rests by his side and opens it. He has already told me nothing comes between him and his god. He says he will pray for me; asks if he can read to me. Why not, I think. He can begin the preparations for the imminent reunion with his saintly wife. In a ritual of seeming self-flagellation, he incants a long passage about adultery that includes casting off limbs into the ocean. All very disquieting. Fundamental. I am glad I don't sew or take my children to Sunday school, but I know I will miss him; so much so that he will have to be tightly locked away, to be taken out only occasionally, otherwise I might go mad. He has changed the chemistry in my brain. We fall asleep. Somehow.

Despite the heavy curtain that blocks out all light and the thick glass that insulates the room from any sound, outside the sun rises and day creeps in. You cannot fight the inevitable. Odd, how we never really know how we will react to any given situation. He is leaving. I am leaving. Our lives will soon follow different trajectories; like drops of water falling from a bottle.

Countdown. Dressed. Packed. Ready.

How do I manage to keep my composure, I wonder. How do I manage not to beg him to stay – to stay with me and make plans for the future?

It's Saturday morning; 9 June 2007. Seven o'clock. It's time.

How very strange that we will both be in Dubai later today. He will arrive hours before I do. By that time he will be reunited with his wife, both of us en route to our real lives, our contracts finished, our neat little worlds packed up and exported back to the far corners of the earth – just a magic carpet ride away.

Unprompted and unexpectedly he grabs me, holds me close to him and hugs me.

'I really like you, Heidi.' He seems to aspirate my name.

'I like you too.' Bizarre. I like you too. Did I really just say that? It's like some kind of involuntary reaction, like Tourette's. I know there is no point in saying anything else. I like you. I have had the wisdom of a sage during this whole thing, surprisingly. He is going back. Leaving. That is inevitable.

Now.

He flashes his huge Antipodean smile. Dimples, always those damn dimples. He gives nothing away. No panic – just self-contained, self-reliant, confident, arrogant, sure. This is the man who prayed to God to make him capable of love – an emotion that didn't come naturally – and to give him some humility.

111

He picks up his duffel bag and hoists it over his shoulder with an ease that emphasizes that he is an alpha male and proud of it, especially in contrast to his rather intuitive, communicative side. He opens the door. The door to the room where we have spent our last night, the very last night. No more maybes; no more dates.

He smiles, again, and turns to leave. He walks past the bathroom, across the landing and heads towards the stairs.

Does he turn again? I can't remember. I watch for a second, maybe two, as he goes, and then I turn away. I don't hear the goodbyes to his colleagues. I don't hear the front door shut. I don't hear the car pull away.

I can't admit it, not out loud, but I know that this is it. He will never again laugh at my idiotic queries or give me lessons on how to drink water from a bottle. I know. Of course, I have always known.

I put on my lip gloss and gather up my things. I take his plastic dog tags and put them in my bag like some sacred amulet, pretending somehow that they connect us.

The house, Nathaniel's house, is now empty, except for the disapproving cook lurking downstairs. I think back, not to a flood of memories, but just to this one small thought, this thing that intrigued him: long ago, he asked where the love goes. It doesn't go anywhere, I told him confidently. He couldn't quite grasp that it just is.

Maybe the truth is different. Maybe it is more like drops of water falling from a bottle, dissolving into space.

8. Dude, Where's My Car?

Jenner drinks way too much. Vodka, mostly. But in 2005, it doesn't seem to matter. The Taliban have gone, the gold rush is in full swing, everyone in Kabul is into some kind of get-rich-quick scam and Jenner, going through his hippie phase, is dancing on tables, two-stepping his way to the illusory pot of gold that lies somewhere over the Afghan rainbow. Kabul is the Wild West.

Bars and restaurants proliferate, and Jenner, in his loud Hawaiian-print shirt, his two Uzbek sidekicks in tow, dances across all sixty of them, and on to the local den of iniquity – because after the bars and restaurants come the prostitutes and the brothels.

Shaking his hips, arms swinging above his head, he bobs out of the last bar, quietly singing to himself (more whining really) and jingling his car keys. Destination: Jo-Jo's.

The roads – dark and potholed – somehow guide the men along. Jenner is in his white Toyota with the Canadian flag sticker on the fender, and the older of the two Uzbeks, squat, thickset, is in the Lexus, seeking the dim light of a cheap neon sign advertising Chinese food. They screech to a halt when they finally find it – more by sheer luck than any navigational judgement. The Afghan guard, waiting for his interminable shift in the long night to end, listens to wailing music from a radio near his feet. He stubs his cigarette out in the dirt, looks up and motions with his chin that they can go in.

Formica tables and white plastic chairs line both sides of the rectangular room. At the far end stands a wooden desk, and behind that a fish tank with fish that look as depressed as their grim surroundings, swimming round and round in circles, trying to find their way home.

The three choose a table across the room, making as much noise as possible in the empty hall, no doubt once the living room of a prosperous Afghan family. A short, grumpy Chinese man shuffles out. He wears a well-worn, faded-to-grey white short-sleeved T-shirt with small holes around the neck and navy braces that hold up his baggy grey trousers. The top of his bald head shines.

'Three beers,' Jenner slurs.

Arrogant and uninterested, in halting English the man says the kitchen is closed and heads to the frugally stocked fridge near the tank. Jenner thinks he remembers some Mandarin from his time in China, but either the man doesn't understand, or chooses not to, or Jenner is actually speaking Tagalog. One of the Uzbeks makes the secret gesture. Of course, he has no idea if this means anything, but he has listened to the far-fetched stories of his friends.

A big, fat mama-san appears from the dark recesses near the fish tank, and barks: 'You got much cash? Enough for three? Only US dollar.'

Jenner, his long, greasy hair stuck to his temples, wavers, even in his inebriated state. The Uzbeks negotiate, while he considers doing what he has actually never done – paying for sex. At this very moment, he is much more concerned with the extremely pressing issue of whether or not he can remain upright.

As his internal debate increases in volume and incoherence, Jenner follows almost blindly; he is impressed that he has managed to get this far. They proceed up the stone stairs of the darkened house, past a locked door, to where the girls, very young girls – from some remote part of China, probably; trafficked, trapped – sit on heavy red velvet chairs.

Taking a swig of Bud, Jenner announces that they are leaving, turns around and literally marches to the landing.

Fumbling for the rail, he grabs it and instructs his bellyaching Uzbeks to follow. Mama-san shouts, furious, while the girls stare impassively, wistfully even – possibly because, rather than the usual grotesque, clapped-out, grizzled old men, these clients were at least young and handsome. Or perhaps they are simply relieved.

Fuelled by rambling subconscious nostalgia for a Hunter S. Thompson life he has never lived, Jenner lets the younger Uzbek, with a dark black moustache, slide into the driver's seat. The hash, plentiful and strong, mixed with the beer and vodka, has really kicked in and Jenner finds himself weak with suicidal laughter. He tosses the keys to the younger Uzbek. 'You ever driven before?'

Foot down, the Uzbek races the white Toyota to catch up with the Lexus flying ahead. Steering recklessly, he replies, 'Hell, no.'

Just like a bad Vietnam movie, Jenner's fried brain thinks.

Speeding at 120 kph down the airport road, one of the few tarmacked surfaces in the capital, Jenner tries, in what appears to him a rare moment of lucidity, to get hold of the wheel. Instead, the car jumps the kerb, hits the side of a building, bounces to the other side of the street and straight into a ditch, right by the Indian restaurant.

As the smoke clears, tyres still spinning, Jenner and the young Uzbek get out, miraculously unhurt.

On the other side of the road the Lexus is perfectly parked.

'Dude, I think there is something seriously wrong with your car,' says the older Uzbek, a cigarette dangling from his lips and a beer in his hand.

Jenner looks at his car. Everything seems pretty hazy. Was there something wrong with it, he wonders. If there was, what was it? But the thought doesn't last long. He crawls into the back seat and goes to sleep. There is work to be done in the morning. Whenever that is.

9. Not Till I Break All Your Bones

A laminated poster hangs on the wall in a women's shelter in Kabul. It shows an Afghan man in a cool, breezy, light-coloured piran tomban confidently striding ahead of his heavily pregnant wife. Wearing a blue burqa, the woman is burdened down with a small child, whom she carries in one arm while balancing a large plastic bag full of groceries in the other. The image aptly depicts the status imbalance between men and women in Afghanistan.

While I look at the poster, one of the victims of domestic abuse, a woman in her thirties, tells her all-too-sorry tale. Her opium-addicted husband beat her and their children regularly, she says, and spent the little money the family had to feed his habit instead of them. When she was finally able to escape, the peace did not last for long. Her husband found out where she was living. He wants her back, and will not give up, he says – not until he has broken all her bones and driven her to the brink of insanity. She has good reason to be afraid.

The Elimination of Violence Against Women (EVAW) law, which bans twenty-two harmful practices against women, was brought in by the Afghan government in 2009 against fierce opposition. Despite years of gender training and vast amounts of aid money poured in by the foreign community, Afghan society largely resisted the change, even though women's rights were enshrined in the new constitution. I had come to the shelter to write about this glaring disconnect between theory and reality for a Canadian quasi-governmental organization called Rights & Democracy.

In conservative Afghanistan taking problems outside the home is considered shameful. As guardians of family honour, women can face further victimization by engaging the justice system, and in a country where simply looking at a man can lead to death, the presence of a woman in the office of a male lawyer or a judge could leave her open to accusations of adultery. Sex outside of marriage is a crime, regardless of circumstance, even in cases of rape.

Most Afghan women can neither read nor write. Not only are they unaware of their rights, but their capacity to access legal information is very limited. 'If you go to my village, which is only forty kilometres from Kabul,' says Haroun Mir, an Afghan analyst, 'women accept whatever is imposed on them. It is all that they know. The rights women have in the West are something unimaginable to them. It is like asking people who have never tasted fruit to tell you how sweet it is.' For women with little experience outside the home, it is difficult to comprehend what rights are, even when explained by a lawyer. Plus, the lawyers and judges themselves might not actually know what the current laws are, and implementation is difficult, as the government operates in only some of Afghanistan's thirty-four provinces.

In rural areas, the decisions of the *jirgas* and *shuras* – bodies that traditionally resolve family and social conflicts – are dictated by customary practices, and many mullahs think reforms go against Shari'a law. 'Men on the *jirgas* are fundamentalists and know nothing about the law or about Shari'a,' says Humaira Rasuli, Country Director of Medica Mondiale Afghanistan, a German NGO. 'They simply decide what they want to decide.'

Rasuli also highlights the problem of having these two legal systems – a formal and an informal one – that contradict each other. Women who use the formal legal system are caught on two fronts. They are seen as supporting the unpopular Karzai government, as well as challenging the status quo. Secondly, by using these new laws they are also seen as supporting the West, the very instigators of these legal reforms.

Even if women want to access the legal system, the cost can be prohibitive. Someone must be hired to write the brief and the plaintiff must leave her village to go to the district office, which may involve renting a car and losing valuable working days. Plus, says Mir, 'If you don't pay the judge, you are definitely going to lose.'

The international community is also culpable here because it has supported women activists on the one hand, while on the other empowering people in government who don't care about the laws.

'Afghanistan has a very tough landscape,' says Fouz Abdel Hadi, an advisor working with the Ministry of Justice. 'Women are not highly educated and they cannot find jobs, so they do not have the tools to either survive alone or support their families.' So in the end, what does a woman gain if she leaves her home and family? Can she live with the stigma, the shame of being ostracized? Even if she is just a young girl, and not married, she will be seen as a revolutionary – an outsider.

The law, ultimately, is like a tiger without teeth. Men see nothing wrong with their behaviour and so replicate the cycle of violence they grew up with in their own homes. And women learn not to feel. Many believe the miserable state of their lives is their fate and God's will, and think they are in no position to express their needs.

'Women understand that what they go through is terrible, but they have no way to resolve their problems,' says the director of the shelter. 'Moreover, the issue of gender is not a top priority for them when poverty, access to public services, insecurity and unemployment rank even higher.'

Janan Mosezai, who became Afghanistan's ambassador to Pakistan in November 2013, brought a much more positive perspective to the argument surrounding the EVAW law. What he saw was robust debate. 'There were extensive debates on local and national TV and radio,' said Mosezai. 'As complex as the law is, the coverage it got made the issue of family law a topic of discussion at the grassroots level, inside and outside Kabul.' People have to fight for their rights because no one is going to give them to you on a silver platter. 'Nothing is easy in this country, but it's not impossible either,' he concluded.

Mosezai disputed the belief that Afghanistan is solely a traditional society and as a result will not change. When I interviewed him in 2010 he was spending half his time in villages. 'If you spend time with people and listen to them, they open up to you, and they want change,' he said. Will it be easy? 'What is easy in this country?' he asked. Afghanistan is not a lost cause, but there are no quick fixes. 'It requires sacrifices, and you have to commit your whole life to the cause, as well as doing things beyond your comfort zone.'

Maybe those glimmers of hope will turn out to be more than faint shards in the darkness. As they say in Afghanistan: drop by drop a river is formed.

10. In and Out of the Grey Zone

He hunts me down. Trailing me, keeping me in his sights. Since the moment we met at the airport in Kabul. Stalking. Waiting. Like the sniper he is.

We first spoke in the queue to board the flight from Kabul to Dubai. I thought he might come and find me during the three-hour flight. He didn't. I forgot about him, still in shock from leaving Afghanistan and Nathaniel. Then we landed, and he found me.

Eighteen months later

I can already hear the disconnect in his voice. He is in Kandahar and I am in London. I can hear the transformation from the first syllable he utters, the change from man to mercenary – from someone who loves to eat and shop and travel to someone who loves his guns, loves to fight, loves to talk about the enemy and loves to kill. I hear it.

The tonal shift is unconscious as the wall rises higher. The sniper who is hyper-focused takes over his personality, blocking off his emotions and love and desire, as the craving to eliminate the enemy and the need to stay alive take over. This is it. He is in and out of the grey zone.

What has happened, I wonder, to the man I saw only a few weeks ago in London during that dark November weekend? The one who told me about his mother leaving him alone as an eight-year-old, while she went out partying, bringing boyfriends home late at night? Where is the little boy who saw himself floating away in a spaceship? What happened to the same emotionally intelligent man who revealed these hidden feelings for the first time to me – the one who, like me, could not see where he ended and I began?

He talks a lot about death; says he will not be taken alive. He has a pill. He will take that. Says he never feels more alive than when he is there and the bullets fly. That is not unusual. He cannot live without the intense, constant presence of death.

'I won't get caught,' he tells me. 'There is too much anger in me.' What should I make of this? At this point he is invincible; I can hear that in his voice. He has survived too many threats to feel vulnerable.

Another day he writes one of his typical short emails; there is infrequent internet access from the FOB, the base in the middle of nowhere. In it he tells me proudly there were eighteen IEDs on the road he will patrol later that night. He emphasizes the number eighteen, as if I might miss the significance of this alarming tally, the terrifying figure that means, yet again, he might dodge death as the smart, savvy, fierce Taliban fighters try to outmanoeuvre our guys – the Brits, the Americans, the Canadians, the Dutch.

'Come back,' I want to say when we finally have a phone line and can talk. But I know I can't. And the gods are on my side: the line goes dead. I sit and think. What is this man who waits for death, who needs to be 'in the zone'; you can never give yourself up in that game of chance, but I understand what makes him tick. I understand the need for excitement, the exhilaration, the sense of being alive, focused and with purpose. I understand it because I need it too, and I want to outrun and outsmart my fear of death, but it stalks me.

But I don't need him, and I am not sure I even want him.

For over a year I avoid him after that first meeting in Kabul airport. Every time he calls, when he is in London, I tell him I am busy. I manage to ignore and evade him for so long, but he just waits, patiently, slowly, surreptitiously, hunting me down like a sniper. That's his MO. It's no fun when the enemy walks into the camp with hands raised high.

Eventually I am caught, or perhaps I surrender.

The dark side of the force has taken over. 'I can feel nothing,' he says from Kandahar. He used to get a rush, but no more. He says to me that every time he whinges that he's bored, something happens. Yesterday he was complaining about getting paid to watch paint dry. Then the situation outside went to hell as an IED went off. He won't talk about the wounded men and the carnage, not over the phone. Instead, he tells me about the puppy with measles which he had to shoot in the back of the head, and how the other puppy, the one who always scrounges for food, just lay outside his door inconsolable. He picked up the sick dog with a forklift, wrapped him in a blanket and laid him down. The little voice, the one inside Paul's head, wonders why he doesn't feel anything.

I can't tell him. He has been in and out of Afghanistan for too many years, chasing too much adventure, trying to feel alive, as if nothing could happen. This is, of course, crazy. The longer you are there, the more you want, the more you push yourself, the more you need, the more you do. It's a no-holds-barred environment. He is right when he tells me that it brings out the best in him; that's why he is attracted to this place – to all these places; that's why he thrives. 'It's what I admire most in human beings,' he says, 'doing the right thing.' He does the right thing and the situation gives him the opportunity to be tested. It is an endless cycle.

When there is phone coverage, which can be either non-existent or sporadic, we speak.

'Cool,' he says. 'I'm doing well.'

'Are you happy there?' I ask, hoping maybe he will be more communicative than usual.

'Yes. It's going very well, and I am running my own show, so as long as I can I will stay here . . . It's getting very bad on the roads; we've had a few "near misses" in the last week.' You can hear the excitement that cheating death again brings.

'That's not good.' I wonder what he expects me to say, and add, 'When you say "near misses" – were you there? Or was it some other team? Hmmm . . . how do you feel?'

'Good. I'm going to do some shooting training tomorrow. I train every chance I get,' he says.

'I meant about the IED situation. How do you deal with it?' I ask again.

'No worries,' he says in that fatalistic way. 'Let the wheel turn.'

129

'What do you mean?'

'I have prepared my whole life . . . if I am not ready now, I will never be . . . some things you can affect and others you can't.' Paul logic; swamp logic.

'True,' I say. 'Still, it freaks me out.' I buy into the deal.

'Sure it does. It's normal.' He corrects himself. 'You're normal.' Then adds, 'Two ramp ceremonies this week', about the dead soldiers going home.

'It's so sad, and so hard to comprehend,' I reply. It is no longer clear what we are doing in Afghanistan.

'It's the nature of the beast,' he concludes in his matter-of-fact way, as if we are discussing something so much more mundane than death. I still don't comprehend. It's not a grey zone that I can actually grasp, but when I am there, in my Afghanistan, which is not his Afghanistan, it makes more sense. It is what puts meaning and clarity into an otherwise moribund existence.

He is more frustrated than I have heard him for some time, frustrated with the Afghans who do not understand him or do his bidding. Food goes missing, then he receives complaints that there isn't enough food.

He says he is taking his gun with him, and is going to settle with the baker. He tells me that the anger in him is raging, and he wants to shoot someone. It will take all his control not to tell the baker that if he ever cheats him again he will break his legs. Has he passed the point? Has he forgotten that he cannot do that, that he shouldn't do that? After how many kills do men lose the ability to feel?

He tells me a story about a colleague who went on leave to the US, made a surprise visit home to see his kids and found his wife in bed with another man. He got the children out of the house. Then he went back and shot the man. Now he is on death row. It is no wonder these men of shadow armies cause such concern when traditional military values of duty and honour are replaced by greed and adventure.

I am silent.

Las Vegas, May 2009

It's strange to see him again after all this time apart. It's been six months since he was in London, when we first actually spent time together. We had a great few days, and he left. No expectations. Now he feels as awkward as I do.

He has come from Bangkok to meet me. I arrived hours earlier from London. The kiss seems almost formulaic, so instead of staying in the hotel, we head out into the Las Vegas night, past Paris and Venice, New York and ancient

Rome, more places than we will ever see together, to reacquaint ourselves.

Our ten-day road trip through the Wild West along Route 66 starts early the next morning. We have talked about this for months, planned it, cancelled it, rearranged it, broken up over it, got back together, re-planned it and now we are here.

Before we head off that first morning he orders a huge breakfast – or, more accurately, three. It amuses me how much he eats – great, monumental quantities. It doesn't show on his body, though, that once tended to fat as a child, but is now honed and sculpted. A few hours later as we drive out of Las Vegas, down the big, wide highway to Colorado, we are both struck by the countryside that feels so familiar. We could be in Afghanistan – the arid desert, the rocky outcrops, the mountains, the absence of colour. We drive and drive.

The next day Paul has a course, to further sharpen his shooter skills. He failed to mention that this would be part of our holiday. I want to leave. I am so mad I want to be gone by the time he is back, whenever that is. It is strange that I have come all this way to fit into his insane schedule.

The voice in my head says he will never live in my world – ever. I know he is not the man for me. Just as he puts his life on the line for the thrill, seeing if he lives through it, I am putting my emotions on that same line.

The next morning Paul goes off again – that's two days in a row – to talk to Steve, a shooter's shooter, who will train him, perfect his skills, improve his aim. They spend hours talking, exploring his pent-up anger and rage, something Steve spots immediately from Paul's stance, from his walk, from his demeanour; it's something Steve has seen before, and he debriefs Paul about his life. I see it too. Does Paul tell Steve about how he bit a kid's shoulder on his first day of school when he was six, I wonder. Does he tell him about the shocking things he did as a teenager? Out of control. Wild, like a wolf.

Breathing is important to a shooter, Steve tells me when I meet him the next day, after bumping into them at Trader Joe's. Psychology is an important part of shooting properly. 'The body is nothing without the mind,' he says. Steve personifies everything about a certain type of roughneck American that I find alien – as alien as if I were in Afghanistan. Here the talk is of moral codes, of men protecting women, of aliens – and not from outer space, but other Americans, invading their territory.

Early the next morning, Steve and Paul grab coffee at Trader Joe's café in Montrose County before they go anywhere near the range. Paul can talk, and he has impressive insight into what makes him who he is and how he got there. Again, they talk for hours.

When Paul goes off, I am left behind in the hotel. Alone. During *our* time together. He has turned off his phone and I have no idea where he is. I cannot stay in the hotel. I ask the sweet girl at the front desk where I should go. Girls in Montrose County seem to have delicate, intricate flowery tattoos. She offers to take me to the coffee house a few minutes' drive away, but I opt for a cab and coincidentally end up at Trader Joe's, where I bump into them.

Later, Paul and I follow Steve to Starvin' Marvin's to have lunch. Our conversation roves, but I can tell Steve is wary of me. He'd be a whole lot warier if he knew I was a journalist, but I am not here on business – this is my holiday . . . a holiday in hell, perhaps, but a holiday. He tells me of his time in Alaska, when it was minus 35°F. He had one light bulb, he traded with Indians for food, he chopped his own wood for the fire to heat the house. 'You don't need more than that,' he tells me.

Oh, yeah? 'Yes, you do,' I say.

With lunch done, we head to the range, where he watches Paul shoot, corrects him, talks to him, explains to me what is happening. Paul practises in the May rain, on the windswept range.

Part of the time I watch Paul perfect his technique through the window of the car as it's freezing outside. I am taking copious notes, writing down my conversations with Steve and my thoughts. I hide my notebook under Paul's kit, and like a duck in a fairground game walk back and forth between the car and the makeshift metal hut where Steve stands, so we can talk and I can understand what he is teaching Paul, what the philosophy is.

Paul lies on the ground, wearing his homemade camouflage gear. When he finishes he gets up and asks about the way his arm should be cocked. To shoot well you need to balance good hand and eye coordination with a sound mind.

I want to know what makes Paul tick, what wires him to this weird world. At his core is the need to do good, to take control, to pare down the hypocrisy of the world we live in, of the politics and politicians. To be apart, different, outside, free. In these interactions there is no 'bullshit'. I hear that a lot. 'When you pull a man, your comrade, out of a ditch, and save his life, you know you have done the right thing, when he depends on you, and you step up to the challenge.' That comes up again and again. Doing the right thing. With me Paul does not talk about killing, the grey zone. Do mercenaries look better in Afghanistan, I wonder – out of place as they are in the urban landscape; out of place, ludicrous.

Paul doesn't mind if he gets killed, which is why he takes these suicide missions. But he tells me I am wrong when I say he doesn't value his life. 'I do,' he responds, standing like a flamingo – one leg wrapped around the other, balancing, aiming, shooting, talking to me while Steve unwraps his prize possession, another big gun.

Paul has no fundamentalist beliefs, but wears amulets to protect him and has mystical tattoos from exotic lands he has visited. These protect him. He has renounced the Catholic faith of his childhood. He constructs his own religion, but cannot lose the spirituality of his past. A Cambodian monk made him a shirt that he wears to save him from harm. With Steve, he has sought out the master.

A lot goes into keeping up gun skills, I learn. Steve brings out handgrips and gives Paul the first one, and the second one to me. I can't squeeze it. Paul tries the toughest one – 190 pounds – and tries to press it between his finger and his thumb. He can't do it.

'Do I need to dump him?' I ask Steve, who effortlessly squeezes it with the might of a man who understands it's his duty to protect women. He laughs. That's what gets him to ease up a bit and let me into this secret world.

Steve says he will let me shoot, and asks if I have ever held a gun. 'No,' I answer, surprised that he would even ask. What kind of girl does he think I am?

'Who protects you in London?' he asks, after I proudly

announce it is illegal for us to have guns.

'Who protects me in London?' I think about this for the first time in my life. I don't live in the Wild West, I tell him, or, for the time being, in Afghanistan. 'London is a reasonably safe place,' I answer, and add lamely, 'The police.'

He shakes his head.

As the hours pass and the evening hastens, a strip of sunlight breaks on the horizon, brightening up the western sky. I retreat to the car and leaf through the two catalogues that lie on the seat beside me. LaRue Guns: 'Made dead-center of Texas, USA.' Dead. Center. As if Texas could be anywhere but America (for now, anyway). Schmidt and Bender USMC do a snazzy-looking sniperscope: 3-12 x 50mm LT – 158 QD mount with Troy BUIS Rear.

Meanwhile, outside, the lesson continues. Paul lies prone on the ground behind a rock. All I can see are his feet sticking out.

Mercifully, the course ends and we leave Colorado. Our trip then begins in earnest, through the Black Canyon and on. We both react to the jagged rocks and waterfalls in the same way, again. We have both done the drive from Kabul to Jalalabad. The similarities strike us simultaneously. From Nevada to Colorado through Texas and on to Arizona, past monster wind farms and places in New Mexico that Paul swears are more dangerous than parts of Afghanistan, areas where he won't stop. Afghanistan. It is in both our souls somehow.

Mile after mile, Colorado slips into the distance. How does he see himself, I ask, in my inquisition.

'It's about who values me,' he answers. 'When your buddies know you and value you. They give you their trust. I have the opportunity to give something back to my pals. It's a gift. It's also about having a moral compass. It is about clarity of purpose, plus it's addictive. Exhilarating.'

His ex-army buddies call Paul 'Wolverine'. I like how he talks, and explains things, and his swamp stories. He fears failing his comrades; everything else is subjugated to that. Everything: the rage, the anger. 'When life is in the balance, the question is: what do I do? How do I protect myself?' This is his unbreakable bond to his brothers. That will always be more important than any relationship. If they need him, he will be there; he will drop everything. Everything. Including me. Or whoever comes after me.

On we go, past ghost towns and tumbleweeds, past churches and boarded-up buildings, past people who trudge to the lone store in pyjamas, in cities that have no more life, no more expectations, no more hope. We talk. The talk is of Afghanistan. We listen to the security contractors' anthems, songs from Linkin Park, as well as their musical collaboration with Evanescence. 'Bring Me To Life' rocks in the background.

We cross another border, this time to see an old Rhodesian tracker, a man more nuanced than Steve – someone who knows the world, who knows the bush, who can ambush. I cannot believe that Paul has scheduled another course with yet another teacher to further improve his skills. He has done this tracker course before, and has sought out another master.

Paul tells the Rhodesian about 'his Afghans' and how they whine about everything. 'They make so many excuses when it is their shift.' I find few things more off-putting than to hear Paul talk so disparagingly about Afghans. He shouldn't be there if that's what he thinks, I tell him.

But in a few weeks he will return, so not worth labouring the point. He is getting ready, slowly, getting into the zone. He has let his beard grow; it suits him, filling out his narrow chin that squeezes his jaw and makes his bottom teeth crooked. He tells me that even the locals in Kandahar get confused because he looks so much like a native.

He laughs at me when I say I can't wait to get back to Kabul. That's not the field; that's a holiday camp, he says.

The field is Kandahar. Again I think my Afghanistan is not his Afghanistan. My Kabul is not his Kandahar.

Every day we drive. Thousands and thousands of miles in less than two weeks, hour after hour, past some of America's most incredible scenery, which is all new to me, new, vast, virgin territory.

At 13:50 Mountain Time we cross into New Mexico, the Land of Enchantment, and on the radio we listen to a debate about Afghanistan. We are in 'God' country, and it is surreal. In this part of the States liberals represent the devil – they are the embodiment of the Antichrist. Here liberal colleges are the very definition of hotbeds of dangerous left-wing communist un-American activity; here homosexuals are misguided and their pernicious behaviour heralds the end of the world. All this Obama liberalism is simply the slippery slope that leads to hell and we are on a collision course. Every time a caller to the station makes a point – it's good to kill abortion doctors – the presenter says, 'God bless you guys'; here, where people 'live for Christ'. Shows how little the Taliban know of godless America. On this station it's common to hear phrases like 'You are dishonouring God' and 'Praying that you are continuing to be portraits of grace'.

It's right what Paul says about this. 'It helps you make sense of life; absolutes are so convenient.' Here and there. Again, the parallels. Across the New Mexico border from Borger we pass Zuzax, en route to Albuquerque (it could be Gardez) and further on to Acoma Pueblo, 120 kilometres west. The rock formations bear a striking similarity to those along the way to Spin Boldak.

On this multi-layered journey of discovery, Paul admits he is self-centred, living outside the system, paying no tax, having no mortgage, purchasing in cash what he needs. To be a sniper is to be a thinking man – it is to outwit the enemy, to pit his life against his enemy's, to see who wins. In this thinking man's game all the skills come into play, attention to detail is vital and keen observation the arbiter of life and death. Stillness . . . you imagine stillness, but there is none in Paul's soul.

Back in Vegas, the last day of our trip, he gives me lessons on staying alive. We practise driving in the empty car park in front of a Wal-Mart. Lessons for future reference – for when I go back to Afghanistan. He makes me curl up in the front seat, still wearing my seatbelt: the same brace position you would assume in an airplane emergency.

'It's common sense,' he tells me. 'If there's an ambush and the bullets are flying, bombs are going off, what do you do if the driver's shot, wounded or dead?' I have no idea. 'If he's a local, you push him out the door; otherwise, use his legs to drive.' I have to take Paul's leg and pick up the dead weight with one hand, steering with the other. 'You have to be aware of your surroundings, master them, be in control.' He tells me I have to be able to do this from the back seat as well. I have trouble lifting his leg. It's heavy, moving it from the brake to the gas, pushing down to stop and go. 'Now reverse,' he says. It's even harder – and academic, he points out, if the car's not automatic. And it's unlikely that it would be.

The car park in Las Vegas feels like Spin Boldak too. The sun sears through the car window and scorches the skin. It is desert hot, and there is a stillness in the air. The kind I find oppressive.

More lessons. I don't want more lessons. This is not how I see the world.

'Go off the beaten track, cross the wrong street and the trouble could be terrifying,' he warns. He is talking about Vegas, London, Toronto. He cautions me to lock the door when he isn't around. His determination takes no notice of the fact that I would prefer to do this later.

'Where's north?' he asks, and is surprised that I can actually identify it from the position of the sun, pleased when I can do it from the way the shadow falls. He'd be more impressed if he knew how totally dreadful my sense of direction is. 'You need to buy a compass,' he tells me.

Then he provides me with a list of essentials for travel – even in the US. This includes a flashlight, which I didn't bring – 'I knew you would have one,' I say; 'Not good enough,' he admonishes. 'And the compass is important if you need to tell someone your coordinates.' I learn that I have to be aware of markers – 'But I'm a trained observer,' I joke. This is no joking matter, though. I need to be able to track distance. 'Make sure your driver arrives with a full tank of petrol.'

I try to compute everything. Leaving the car is like breaking the seal, he tells me. I need to look at the three coordinates, my ring of protection. This lesson in the Wal-Mart car park takes place on the way to the gun store, the first I have ever been to, and probably the last too. He has decided we need to sort this out. In Afghanistan everyone carries a gun. 'But they don't know how to use it,' says Paul. 'And here they are just freaks,' he says. 'At least gun laws in Canada are not so different, but the mentality is. It's white trash here, the same pool they recruit from for the army. In Canada, it's a better class, and that's why we have better soldiers.'

The queue at the gun shop for the range proves too long, and anyway I don't really want to do this. But we come close when we go to see the just-premiered *Star Trek* movie the next day. We play a video game where we have to shoot the moving human targets in the jungle, and it is difficult.

'Reload,' Paul instructs me, almost shouting. I have no idea what the hell he is talking about. I can't figure it out. Reload, I am thinking. It takes me a minute to clue in that as we play and terminate the targets in the video jungle I need to reload my video gun. It's exciting trying to figure out where the threat is coming from, to work out who has a gun, not knowing who is going to strike next, not being trigger-happy in case you shoot the hostages, assessing who might emerge from deep cover, who might get you.

'Money and adventure. What could be better?' His mantra. He's right, and I understand. I also score higher than he does. Maybe I have a greater natural ability. I understand the glamour of war (despite knowing the overwhelming horrors), the excitement, the emotions it stirs, the adrenalin, the action, the adventure, the stories, the courage and all the paraphernalia – but I see it from a safe distance, peering in.

In a week he will be back in Kandahar.

There are many Pauls in Kabul, and maybe I have had enough for one lifetime, dipping into this alien world where

I do not belong. Maybe it is time to go home, to leave this grey zone and adventure behind. This is my life, after all, not a story.

He calls me from the plane. The restaurant where I am in London is modern and noisy and I can hardly hear what he says. I try to find somewhere quiet, keeping the conversation easy and light. The plane to Dubai will take off in a few minutes, and tomorrow he will fly directly to the base. He tells me that this season IED attacks are predicted to increase by 50 per cent. Then the line goes dead.

This man who talked to me at the airport in Kabul as we boarded the flight to Dubai two years ago has left again. Vegas–Bangkok; Bangkok–Dubai; Dubai–Kandahar. Back into the spaceship that transports him to another world, far away. Slipping in and out of the grey zone.

11. A Girl with no Borders

Kabul, 2009

Hasina bounded down the expansive staircase like a force of nature, coming to a shuddering halt beside me before flinging herself both onto the ottoman and into the conversation – all without missing a beat.

Two green cut-velvet sofas, which stood opposite each other on the marble floor, were separated by a low glass-top coffee table with incongruous gold dolphins as legs. Humayoun made an extravagant gesture indicating I should sit. A fiercely proud Pashtun, he had been a colleague of mine in 2007, when I first arrived in Kabul.

I immediately liked Humayoun's cousin, Hasina, but almost immediately stopped liking Humayoun himself, as he tried to prove that the gender gap had closed in Afghanistan and all was well with the world.

'Yet, despite our cultural differences,' he insisted, in his formal explanation, 'men and women are now treated equally; Afghanistan', he reassured me, 'has come a long way.'

Hasina butted in. 'How can you say that? They are not equal.' The Kabul University student turned to me: 'You know that for my research I worked with widows. I worked at an international NGO distributing food. I have heard these women's stories and I can tell you as an Afghan woman, there is no equality, and definitely not for the poor and destitute.'

I looked over at Humayoun, feeling as though I was observing a ping-pong match, my head bobbing back and forth.

'You're wrong, Hasina *jan*,' he said quietly, an air of barely restrained menace in his voice.

Soon afterwards, Humayoun excused himself and went upstairs.

As we sat together, I told Hasina I would love to meet up with her – alone, without her intrusive cousin, so that we could talk frankly. I invited her to my 'villa', as these Afghan houses were called. I was staying nearby. We hastily arranged to meet the next day at 11 a.m., then continued to chat until Humayoun reappeared.

'There's a call for you – you need to take it,' he instructed Hasina.

Soon after I too excused myself, went to the loo and, taking a small piece of paper from my notebook, wrote my name, address and mobile number on it. I folded it up and put it in my pocket.

Hasina had not returned.

Before leaving I asked Humayoun if I could say goodbye to his cousin, as I didn't want to seem rude. He called for her and, when she appeared, he did not take his eyes off her. I slipped the paper surreptitiously into her hand as we kissed each other goodbye.

The next day I waited. She never appeared.

Twenty-three years ago Hasina's mother was distraught to find that she was going to have yet another child. She already had three daughters, and at five months pregnant the doctor told her it was too late for an abortion. He calculated the child's birth would be on Teachers' Day – significant because Wadjma was both a teacher and a mujahid, who fought against the Soviets. 'You will have a revolutionary daughter,' he predicted.

True to the doctor's prophecy, Hasina was never very obedient, nor was her mother ever reconciled to the fact that she wasn't the longed-for son. Growing up, Hasina would run around like a wild thing and her mother would tell her how disappointed she was at having had another girl. But Hasina would think to herself, 'What good luck you had that it was me!' She was indeed a revolutionary daughter.

Hasina was born as the civil war broke out in Afghanistan, and revolution came at a high price for her family. During the early nineties, her father's six brothers were killed one by one, until he eventually went crazy with grief. Hasina remembered the stories he told her, years later, of the terrifying knocks on the door at night, of the times he had been arrested, detained and questioned. 'He had cheated death so many times,' she said ruefully.

One time her father had been taken to prison. Crouching in a cell full of prisoners, he had seen an old childhood friend pass by, dressed in uniform. As small boys these two men had walked to school hand in hand, and as they grew older they'd remained very close until they had eventually gone separate ways. The man in the uniform did not acknowledge his old friend, but Hasina's father saw him glance at him out of the corner of his eye. Within days, he was released, but when he returned it was to an empty home; while he was imprisoned, the family had left for Pakistan. He knew his luck was ebbing away. At some point, he reckoned, one group or another would come for him. And if they didn't get him, the mortar shells destroying the city and killing so many surely would.

Meanwhile, his family had trekked for nine days and nights over the Hindu Kush, ploughing through snow and ice like millions of other refugees. Hasina's small sisters had held on to their mother's coat. Hasina was just four months old.

By the time she saw her father again, Hasina was no longer a baby. A strange man arrived at the door, which Hasina opened, and upon seeing him she had gone running and screaming to her mother, thinking the enemy had come to their house. They had been warned not to speak to strange men because the family had many political enemies. The older girls didn't recognize their father either.

The war had taken its toll, and he had retreated totally into himself, languishing for months afterwards in a dark room in their house, his dreams shattered. He had lost his country and his brothers, and what remained of his family could barely eke out a living. He was rendered powerless. For a very long time the children believed the curious man was just a relative who had nowhere else to go. He was so broken he couldn't even deal with his own children.

Kabul, 2010

Hasina wore big Gucci sunglasses as she sat sipping coffee at Flower Street Café in central Kabul. Not quite what

I'd expected to see. The twenty-two-year-old underground activist who aspired to emulate India's 'Bandit Queen', Phoolan Devi, had called up the shop in Rome and talked them through the sunglasses she wanted: dark lenses and wide frames. They couriered the package to her.

I didn't recognize her at first, I must be honest, as she sat staring at me in the café. She was slim and fashionable, reluctant to wear her hijab, which always slipped off her long, shiny black hair, settling quite naturally on her shoulders as she talked animatedly. Her excellent English was learned in Pakistan.

'I know you,' she said, arriving at my table on her way out. I drew a blank, but didn't want to appear rude. I smiled vacantly.

'I met you with my cousin Humayoun.'

'Yes,' I responded. Stunned. Yes, I suddenly realized who it was. I couldn't believe it. 'How are you?' She hugged me. We both smiled.

Over the following months we would meet at this café, one street away from my house, on a regular, sometimes daily, basis. During this time she told me her incredible story. I loved listening to her. She was so vibrant, so full of life, so much fun, so inquisitive, so unafraid, so determined, so feisty, so infused with a desire to change the world for women in Afghanistan – so unlike the stereotypes of Afghan women. It occurred to me that we should write a book, and at one of our numerous meetings I mentioned this. My remark was met with silence, and then she said, 'I am not interesting.' But we talked for a while, and then she exclaimed the idea is 'very fantastic'. I love the way Afghans say that. Very fantastic indeed.

We also started to meet at my house, a bungalow built in the 1960s, which needed some tender loving care. We attracted less attention there. Everything is watched in Kabul – by someone. The big garden was home to two rabbits. At first we thought they were in love as they could never be apart. Every time we looked over they were canoodling. Then we discovered that one of them was a bully and would not leave the other alone. The sweet rabbit sought peaceful sanctuary, where he could be alone without being terrorized, but in vain. I took to feeding them whole carrots, although if I could have only fed the nice one I would have. The bully jerked the carrot out of my hand and ran off to eat it; the gentle rabbit would chew the carrot while I held it. Another obvious metaphor.

One day Hasina brought two of her sisters to the house. We sat in the garden near the pomegranate tree, where the rabbits liked to go, and we relaxed on the large bench, beautifully designed by Rahim Walizada, a very talented Afghan artist, chatting in the cut-crystal clarity of the magical Kabul light. We talked about curtains and fashion . . . and a rampant fungal infection that Hasina was suffering from.

Hasina's siblings are not cut from the same cloth as their youngest sister. They don't have her spirit, her radical disposition and, like many women here, they are happy to conform to the customs of their society. They want to get married, have children, be part of life, to follow the conventions they know and understand, to play by the rules. To stay alive. More like Humayoun, who had, it transpired, taken the paper I had pressed into Hasina's hand and thrown it away, warning her not to meet me.

Hasina is more like her grandmother: the grandma who always stood and never sat. 'She made me who I am today,' said this formidable young woman who has no fear of death. 'I remember in the refugee camp in Pakistan, she would tell me stories at night when I was a little girl and we curled up together in bed. Every once in a while, during her tales, she would climb out and feed me sweets from her secret cupboard as I drifted in and out of sleep.'

As she grew up, Hasina listened to her grandma talk about her life, and the immutable sadness she suffered when her husband took another wife. 'It destroyed her to the core of her being,' she told me. She had loved this man, her father's father, but had no power to prevent him from marrying again, and to a woman he ended up loathing as much as she ended up loathing him.

'In my heart I have divorced her,' he would tell Hasina about her other grandmother: the one who only sat.

Her grandma's sadness started when her own parents died. She was only a small child, and it was left to her uncles to bring her up. Despite her always wanting an education, her family didn't believe in sending girls to school. Instead, they married her off when she was sixteen to a man ten years older.

'I asked her if she was happy,' said Hasina. But this was not a concept that factored into her grandma's life. 'It didn't matter,' she told Hasina. Her husband made her work hard, gave her barely any money and never paid attention to her needs. And he would beat her. Despite this, she loved him.

Hasina would listen, tears in her eyes, thinking she would never have survived this. 'She always took a serious interest in my education,' Hasina said. She wanted her granddaughter to achieve what she had been unable to.

'People say that I hate men and that I am a feminist, but I am not against men. But since I heard my grandma's stories of how my grandpa tortured her, it has affected me.' Almost every Afghan household runs along this basis.

As a child in Pakistan, Hasina studied at a RAWA school. The Revolutionary Association of Women of Afghanistan remains a fairly marginalized, Maoist-inspired group that instructed women to wear men's clothing as a means of promoting gender equality, but still stuck to a male agenda.

Hasina refused. 'What does wearing men's clothing have to do with equality?' she challenged her infuriated teacher. 'I'm not a man, so why should I wear men's clothing?' She loved fashion, even then.

RAWA seemed to disenfranchise the very people they sought to engage; their language was too elite and alien, which was one reason Hasina never joined their ranks as an adult. What RAWA did, however, was to identify Hasina's innate leadership skills, which they cultivated. At five years old Hasina and her young classmates would talk about politics. Her campaign to change women's lives began then, as a child.

At ten years old Hasina wrote a poem called 'A Girl With no Borders', about a child who had no restrictions in her life, no borders to separate her from her family, her land, her thoughts, her freedom and the world. Her imagination was also fired by RAWA magazines; it was in their pages that she read about Phoolan Devi and determined to follow her Indian heroine's example. As she grew older, it began to crystallize for Hasina that there was no internal core to the nascent women's movement in Afghanistan, no grassroots stirrings, no countrywide desire for change. There were a few well-known female role models and some female leaders throughout Afghanistan's history, but not many. There was also no obvious way to have influence in the male networks where deals were brokered.

At twelve, Hasina moved back to Afghanistan to join her parents, now based in Herat. Remembering her grandma's words, she decided to educate girls. She started a small school in the basement of her aunt's house, with only four cousins. In the four years she was there, it grew.

'The more cities I saw, the more I understood the problems of women in my country. The situation gave me more and more energy to fight the system, to fight for my rights, to fight for my humanity. Every night I would think of ways to change this predicament,' she told me.

As the doctor once predicted, Hasina's mother had indeed produced a revolutionary daughter, and during her second year at university, Hasina was kicked out. She had taken her student protest a little too far, organizing campaigns against male professors who sexually harassed female students, promising good grades and pass marks in return for sexual favours.

Rather than sit around, Hasina went to Kandahar to research sex. Amazingly, given what we know of the Taliban and conservative Afghan culture, sex was thriving, and so was the sex industry. The sex trade in Afghanistan has always been alive and well.

Hasina felt like a criminal for being female, walking the streets of Kandahar, where men shut their women up behind high walls and barricades. Her mission was to research how women felt about sex, about sex on the first night after they got married, what they knew about sex before they were married, where they learned about it, what they thought of their husbands. 'I was shocked by what I found out,' she told me. 'Women were having sex whenever the opportunity arose, and not just with their husbands.'

One married woman would wait by the window to signal to her neighbour that the coast was clear. Another girl, protected by her older sister, courted a boy in the attic of the family house. The young man would crawl along the rooftops and slip in through the girls' window. Their parents imagined they were just talking in the cool night air, which blows the desert dust away. Hasina lived with the family during her research and was slowly let in on the secret. She asked to meet the boy.

'Oh, he is so handsome,' the girl said to Hasina, but when Hasina met him she didn't think he was handsome at all. She knew what this young woman thought about the boy, but what did the boy think about the woman who risked everything for him?

'Do you love Khalida?' Hasina asked.

'No,' he said, bluntly, and right in front of the girl.

'So why do you have sex with her?' Hasina asked, bewildered.

'I am a man and I just wanted to play with her, and she asked for it.'

Hasina was shocked. 'If there is no true love, how can you do this?' she asked. She would have dumped him faster than you can say Gucci. Love is a crime in Afghanistan, Hasina would remind me during our frequent discussions.

'I have asked myself if being born in Afghanistan is the worst deal in the world. Was it my destiny to be born in a country where I, a woman, am considered no better than an animal? We need to fight for our rights because no one else is going to do it for us,' she said, still believing in the possibility of change. 'But women have to take responsibility to change the situation. No one is responsible for our rights except us.'

Hasina was particularly drawn to the plight of widows. In the misogynistic culture that pervades all Afghanistan, women without husbands are the lowest unfortunates on the trash heap of life. Hasina decided that to convince the widows she was on their side, she must live the way they lived. She ate the same dirty nan that they ate. For weeks she did not brush her teeth. 'These women know nothing of dental hygiene. Even if they did, they have no running water. Maybe it wasn't the best thing to do as I still have problems with my teeth and gums, but for them to believe me, to trust me, I felt I had to do this.'

Hasina had met many such women when she worked at the distribution centre of an international aid organization, which supplied them with monthly rations. In 2003 Anita Anastacio from Mercy Corps started a project building houses on an empty Kabul hillside. The women also cooked mantu, a popular meat dumpling, which they sold at nearby schools. It was not a new idea, but one that worked. The rations got them through the day, but what Hasina learned was that only the women themselves could alter their fate.

So under the auspices of Mercy Corps, Hasina became part of a group initiating informal associations, gathering ten women together every week to see if they could find solutions to their own problems. The first group discussed the very unhappy situation of a woman who wanted to get divorced, but who, like so many women here, couldn't for myriad reasons – not least because she lacked the necessary skills to survive on her own. Divorce also brought shame, shame brought alienation, alienation brought distance from family, including children. The solution often wasn't any better than the problem.

Even before Hasina was born her future had been predicted – after all, it is destiny that most people here cite for their circumstances.

Left to her own devices, Hasina would run around naked, a paradox in a culture that views nudity as *haram* (impure). Shame is, of course, attached to everything, and particularly to everything a woman does, says or sees. For Hasina one word, *sharm* (shame), holds women down like pinned butterflies. 'Being naked connects me to the soil, to my emotions, to life and to freedom.' A girl with no borders.

In a tightly regulated culture, Hasina lives for emotion. How, she would wonder out loud, could she be her mother's daughter? 'Nothing by the name of emotion is important to my mother. She always obeys my father and is proud of it, even though she too is university-educated. For me, the

160

worst thing that could have happened to my mother was to marry my father.'

At university, the same one her parents went to, Hasina made two very close friends. Amina and Masouda were as different in looks as they were in thought. Amina was much more conservative, with no intention, inclination or desire to change, happy to follow the tenets of Islam and proud to conform to the strictures of her society – something I continue to find difficult to comprehend. She was quite beautiful – tall, slender and elegant, with high, moulded cheekbones, almond-shaped eyes, full lips and airbrushed skin. She wore her cream scarf with mink pompoms wound tightly·around her head, applied like a bandage. It only emphasized the perfect shape of her skull and her sculpted face.

Masouda's plumper, shorter body was covered in turquoise – tight turquoise trousers, a matching hijab with thin lines of silver running through the cheap cotton, worn with a long turquoise top – and she carried coordinating folders for her class notes.

While the graceful Amina would refuse even to look at a picture of the man her parents would ultimately choose for her to marry, Masouda was boy-crazy, no different from young women in the West. She was transfixed by Hasina's openness, honesty and candour.

When I met with the three of them, I had to check my surroundings to make sure that I was still in Afghanistan, as Masouda told the rest of us about her love life. The girls were being updated, and I was thrown in at the deep end. She was having an affair with one of her professors, an Afghan who was, of course, married, with a family in Australia. Masouda was labouring under that universal illusion that he loved her and would leave his wife and family to live with her in Afghanistan. Just in case, though, she had her eye on someone else – a boy she often called and talked to. This made Hasina furious and she chastised her friend.

'Stop calling him,' she instructed, with typical passion. 'If he wants to talk to you, he knows your number.' The Rules are The Rules everywhere, it seems. Hasina then further disabused her friend of any illusion that this other boy would ever marry her, telling her that his family would choose his bride. 'And it won't be you,' she said with characteristic clarity.

Masouda thought she was being so clever, but both Amina and Hasina worried about her, and for good reason. That kind of behaviour could get you killed by your own family.

Our conversation took place on the university campus, behind one of the buildings that on this particular afternoon was empty. Hardly any students passed by, but occasionally one or two boys turned when they saw the four of us hidden away. The greenery and the light were as beguiling as ever.

'Over there was a mass grave,' Hasina told me, pointing to a plot of scrubland. 'Kabul suffered so much during the war; every metre of this land is a person's final resting place.'

Then, returning to their conversation, Masouda and Amina discussed why Afghan girls deny that they have any desire, and decided it is because they worry what others will say, and that it all comes back to shame.

'Girls don't really understand their own desire,' Hasina pronounced. 'Are Afghans different from other people? No, but they are afraid, and no one talks to them about what is going on and what happens, so they don't really know.'

Did they know more in the past, when Afghanistan was supposed to be more open and women wore miniskirts, I wondered.

After many months of inspiring, joyous meetings with Hasina, everything suddenly changed. Her sisters were now engaged and a wild child could not be allowed to tarnish the family's honour. She was given a 'companion'. Forced upon her by her family, this dour, black-robed chaperone shadowed Hasina everywhere like a phantom bodyguard and I never saw my friend alone again.

Hasina could no longer meander on her way home from university and meet me at Flower Street Café or introduce me to her friends. She no longer let the headscarf slip casually from her hair, now cut to her shoulders. She no longer had male friends with whom she would hang out in places she would take me to, where we would talk and drink tea.

She lost her Gucci sunglasses and her phone. And she lost her freedom. It was not even possible to slip a note into her hand as I had done at her cousin's house. The strict guardian of Hasina's virtue never let a second pass without her laser glare searing through her young charge. They were like split amoebas; two halves of a whole, cleaved together. Over the months that I remained in Kabul, I occasionally ran into Hasina – at the supermarket, at a café – but the three of us would simply nod and walk on.

On one of my last days in town, I saw Hasina and the black-clad overseer sitting and drinking coffee. We exchanged hellos and I was allowed to join them. Hasina had recently managed to get a new phone, which pinged her a message. She read it.

'What is it?' demanded her guardian.

Her best friend from high school had been found murdered, Hasina reported. The suspect was the girl's mother-in-law.

Before the wicked witch came on the scene, Hasina and I would look at scholarships she might apply for or conferences she could attend. But then it simply became impossible for us to have private conversations. Her family checked her emails and monitored her phone calls. I couldn't have protected her if she'd run away to stay with me. There were no Marines to spirit her away. No safe houses where she could hide. No country, apart from Pakistan, that would accept her. No visas waited for her. There was nothing I could do for her unfinished life before I went back to my own in London, but still I wondered if I could have done more.

Hasina never feared death. She had said this so many times to me, and she may genuinely not have been afraid to die, but I heard the echoes of her murdered heroine Phoolan Devi, and I feared for her.

Yet the truth is, despite everything, she was not so willing to leave. The girl with no borders could never imagine living outside her country, away from her beloved Afghanistan. That was the only border that mattered to her and she had her destiny to fulfil.

12. Cappuccino Capital

A Recipe for Setting up Shop in a Post-Conflict Zone

This is a classic English dish, much loved by those who have romantic notions of exotic lands and following in the footsteps of Lawrence of Arabia.

Ingredients

1. Fabulous connections
2. A new school
3. Very expensive handbags and designer sunglasses
4. Extreme adventure
5. A think tank
6. A taste for bad coffee
7. The List
8. A band
9. Celeb friends
10. Support for women
11. Rescued street dog

Start with: a prince, a president and ancient handicraft

As you have walked alone across the country, for some baffling reason you are now an 'expert'. You have hung out with the locals, eaten their food, slept alongside their sheep, and walked with their goats. You understand that the troops must leave. 'We have no business being in Afghanistan,' you say regularly. You stick to this line.

You happen to know Prince Charles, who knows President Karzai, who likes the idea of starting a school that teaches Afghans what Afghans already know – wood carving, jewellery-making and calligraphy. Modernization may not yet have hit the Silk Road, but your mission is to preserve the ancient, but not lost, arts. You have the best of intentions, and you make a significant contribution to the regeneration of Kabul's old city, but it's also no bad thing when the project turns out to be yet another fabulous platform for your enviably media-savvy persona.

You find an impressive location and renovate the crumbling building. Your famous friends, with names like Violet and Amaryllis – upper-class English girls whose grandfathers ran the colonies – work there. They chronicle their adventures on the prestigious pages of the *Spectator*.

To enormous fanfare you open the school and become the darling of the British press. You are considered a genius and a saviour – talked about as a future prime minister. In fact, you truly are a genius. Movie stars line up to play you and princes and presidents shake your hand.

Stir in: expensive handbags and sunglasses

Every girl needs to look good, even here in Kabul. The markers of success for *Afghanistas* are large, expensive handbags and large, designer sunglasses. These items are not just for footballers' wives and you are able to stock up when you go on your weekend shopping sprees to Dubai. And why not? After all, you are making loads of tax-free money from your vague international consultancy job – although, unlike some people in Kabul, your cash doesn't come in brown paper bags delivered monthly by the CIA.

Add to taste: extreme adventure

It's not enough to live in a war zone, especially if you are French, and especially as you have the Alps on your doorstep back home. What better way to spend a weekend than to go skiing on virgin snow in some far-flung region of Afghanistan? You are so cool you don't care about the unexploded ordnance scattered by the Soviets and the mujahideen. You have become blasé about danger. This is simply one more challenge: you have skied off-piste in Europe, heli-skied in Banff, swept down the mountains of Lebanon during the day only to party by the Mediterranean at night. You have climbed Everest (who hasn't?), but found all those people at base camp tedious – and anyway, you did it years ago on the way from East Timor to Baghdad. Or was it Darfur to Kosovo? Long before it became trendy in any case.

168

Drizzle: a car with a personality

On Friday morning, the start of the weekend, you gather your friends into your VW car, very cleverly named Herb-i-Islami by very clever British journalists (a very clever pun on the name of the political party of Islamist leader Gulbuddin Hekmatyar: Hezb-i-Islami.) You head to Bamiyan, where the giant, ancient Buddhas used to be, before the Taliban dynamited them to smithereens. This is cool in Kabul.

Mix with: a think tank

You tell everyone that you are starting the first real Afghan think tank, with real Afghans, who will give real Afghan opinions, so this will be the authentic voice of the Afghan people. After all, you are here to represent them. You declare yourself to be a 'personal ambassador of goodwill'.

You try not to say 'great white saviour' or mention The Great Game.

Sprinkle on: bad coffee

Bad coffee is drunk in copious amounts at the many cappuccino cafés where you work as the internet there is better than at your home. You are friendly with the guards and you banter away in Pashto or Dari, making sure your warmth with the locals is widely observed.

Whisk in: The List

You work hard, as do your colleagues, and you need to unwind. You organize a huge shindig, which takes months to plan and vast amounts of money. You transform a bleak container-like compound into a *kochi* (nomad) tent, with carpets hung from the ceiling and many more covering the floor. Only people on The List are allowed in. You are on The List, as you have created it. But, surprise, this is not Hollywood.

Heat slowly

While ordinary Afghans try to figure out some way to settle in another country – any country – you settle in. You pal up with a few of the elite, and decide you want to be a rock star in the evenings, when you are not saving the Afghan people by day. The band needs a clever name; you call it Emergency Response. It was called Lockdown, but your celebrity friend said she didn't like that. She flies into Kabul with a couple of Hollywood pals for your gig. You make the news on CNN. You book a tour across the 'Stans. You begin to believe your own PR.

Pour in: support for women

You have to save the women. Women for sure need saving. You have them clean your large house that once belonged to their family before it was stolen by a local warlord while they were refugees in Pakistan, and is

170

now being rented to you. You assure them your NGO, the one that you have just started, will build a school in their village to educate the girls. Everyone builds schools – but what about the teachers to teach there?

You call everyone *jan* (dear), and believe the locals have taken you into their hearts. You are one of the people. You wear a piran tomban, joking with your friends about the 'manjammies'. You put a flat, round woollen pakul on your head so you look like Afghan hero Ahmad Shah Massoud, and wrap yourself in a patoo, a heavy woollen blanket, to ward off the cold air, even in summer. Your hand floats over your heart in the common Afghan greeting, and you always say, solemnly, '*Salaam alaikum*', as if you were born speaking the lingo.

Season with a dash of rescued street dog

You go to Bush Bazaar (latterly named Obama Market) to buy US Army-issue goods that have supposedly fallen off the back of a truck originally destined for the troops. AK-47s and the odd grenade will make exceptional decorations for the bungalow you call home. You debate whether to go up-armour or soft skin and ask your security people for advice. Very cool people have their own Cougar MRAP, a mine-resistant vehicle produced by Force Protection Inc.

You name your rescued street dog after your country's ambassador, a friend of your father's from Eton and Oxford.

Bake

Your Cappuccino Capital is now ready to bake. Put in the oven for thirteen years. Take out in 2014. Leave to cool.

Self-serving.

13. My Work Here is Done

I inherited Dunia.

But not in the way one might expect, like an indentured labourer, as the roles were reversed and I was tied to her in perpetuity.

I was the typical *kharagi* (foreigner), suffering from the kindness-of-strangers syndrome. I wanted to help people. Any people. People less fortunate than myself. Afghans. Any Afghan. And especially any Afghan woman.

We were all so keen to help our Afghan cousins and so many of them were keen to be the recipients of our largesse. They were hardly stupid. We had big, easy money, and they wanted big, easy money. If we were going to give it to them, why shouldn't they take it?

But that wasn't really Dunia's modus operandi. She wasn't greedy; she was heroically lazy – in a league of her own, I like to think. Paid to be our housekeeper, she took the art of doing nothing to a new height.

I blame Gracie Belle.

The first time I met the willowy Gracie, during an interview at the Ministry of Women's Affairs, she struck me as hostile and frightening. First impressions, as I discovered, can be greatly misleading. Gracie Belle possesses a rare spirit of generosity and while she may be brutally amusing, she is rarely, if ever, hostile. And because she wanted to help Dunia in any way she could, I did too.

Dunia had so much potential, which we saw and tried to encourage. She was smart and funny. She had a warm and lovely personality, and was hard to dislike. She had flair, and loathed cleaning. We knew she hated what she was doing, and because of that Gracie did everything she could to try to help her. She paid for Dunia to learn English in the hope that, with improved language ability, she would be able to translate her skills into a better job. That would bring much-needed security for herself and her family.

Dunia, for her part, put up with all of us poking and prodding her to do what we wanted her to do with her life. She magnificently and skilfully resisted all our efforts with good-natured aplomb.

We had agreed that she would come in to work every day, but whether she showed up or not would depend on a variety of things, including the state of traffic, if it was too muddy to wear her new shoes or how many of her relatives had died the previous night. Work was a casual concept at best.

'Oh, Miss Gracie,' she would say, over her Bollywood glitter-covered mobile phone, 'last night my cousin's brother's sister's best friend had to go to hospital and I must stay home.' I'm pretty sure, had I bothered to keep track, the entire nation would have expired by the end of my time in the country.

Of course, Dunia was always able to come to work on the days she was paid, and her salary was guaranteed whether she worked, didn't work or might work at some point in the future. It never occurred to her it might be otherwise. Dunia also expected to be paid extra for Eid, for Ramadan, for Christmas, for the anniversary of her father's death or to buy new clothes for any cousin's wedding – and those always took place during the working day. It was a great gig and one that I was pretty keen on getting myself.

She more or less got away with all this for a very long time – her story was classic, and so the dance of the great white saviours and their needy beneficiary played out between all of us brilliantly.

In a culture in which the vast majority of the population is thin and quite short, Dunia was tall and round and large. She was also Hazara, making her a Shia Muslim, loathed by the majority of Sunni Pashtuns from the south of the country who believed in their own superiority.

With the death of her father, Dunia's prospects of marriage had diminished: not only was she poor, she also had little in the way of a dowry. While not considered attractive, she had a lovely face with beautiful features, and a personality that shone through. But she was getting old (though still only in her early twenties) and she had eight brothers and sisters to care for. Her mother had had a nervous breakdown on becoming a widow and couldn't work; the task of supporting the family had fallen to Dunia.

All the elements were there to claim our sympathy and our help, although what good sympathy did I'm not sure.

And Dunia didn't make it easy . . .

Gracie and I would spend hours looking for clothes that were supposed to have been ironed or, if we were expecting guests, for tablecloths or place mats or napkins, which we could never find. They disappeared for weeks. It was a constant riddle. Where could they be? The house wasn't that big and there weren't that many hiding places.

Mysterious piles of undiscovered laundry lay in darkened corners, collecting dust. Instead of ironing, Dunia would draw the heavy velvet curtains in the living room for privacy and, with the TV blasting, she would practise her best Indian dance routines, copying the glamorous actresses in the over-the-top Bollywood movies she and the rest of the country loved. Much later, she would emerge and say with a flourish, 'My work here is done', before heading off home.

On the plus side, she did enjoy going to the market to do the weekly shop, which also provided her with ample opportunity to top up her own family's groceries. And she enjoyed flirting with the two guards at the house, with whom she held long conversations.

She liked to torment the hard-working *chala* (auntie), who cleaned the house next door, boasting how much more money she made, which was true. The woman who lived next door paid well above local rates, but not the vastly inflated wages so many foreigners overcompensated with, distorting the real economy.

On those rare occasions when Dunia did actually arrive at the house in Taimani, she would take off her long, dark chadori to expose some wonderfully colourful outfits. She had great taste, and if I couldn't decide what to wear, or figure out if something was appropriate or not, she would go through my clothes and match things up, giving me good advice.

The house wasn't particularly large, and Dunia's tour of duty would never take long. It had one bedroom, a small kitchen, a living room and what we referred to as the winter palace – a glass-room extension where I slept, which was freezing in winter and boiling in summer. In the end, there is only so much dancing you can do, and so after a quick circuit round the single-storey house, Dunia would make her usual pronouncement, and I, the stunned foreigner, would just say, 'Sure, OK, fine. See you tomorrow.'

Far less sympathetic were Afghans and friends familiar with Afghanistan, who would not only roll their eyes in despair, but get angry at our indulgence in allowing Dunia to get away with her exploitation of us – a couple of poor, dumb foreigners. Lots of deserving Afghans needed work, like the *chala* next door, for one. 'Fire her,' was their constant refrain. But Gracie and I couldn't bear to do it. After all, it was one reason we were here. We wanted to help women; we were all part of the sisterhood.

When Gracie's new job required her to move out of our shared home, responsibility for Dunia, along with her family, the future of the country and the entire universe fell on my shoulders. I tried to keep my cool with her, thinking that I should be a better person, be more sympathetic to what a rough time this poor Afghan woman had to cope with in all other areas of her life. But my ranting phone calls to Gracie expressing absolute exasperation became more and more frequent, requiring her to calm me – and the situation –

down, which she somehow always managed to do. Patience and grace were two of her great qualities.

Predictably, Dunia got on with doing what she did, and I resigned myself to her continuing presence in my life. For Gracie, Dunia was like a family member. This wasn't time-limited. Gracie's commitment to Dunia and her family was, she felt, for life, for better or worse.

Before leaving for a three-week break, I discussed with Dunia the need for her to clean the house during my absence. I wasn't asking for miracles, but Kabul is incredibly dusty . . . I wanted to know I'd be returning to a habitable environment.

Gracie reinforced the message with Dunia when I handed her my phone. 'So you know, Miss Dunia,' Gracie said, 'Miss Heidi likes the place clean. So you must go every day while we are away. If you have to bring your sisters, you know that's fine. They can watch TV and there is always food.'

'Oh, yes, Miss Gracie, of course. I will be there every day. Please, have a good holiday and Merry Christmas. My family sends you their love.'

In those three weeks, while Gracie and I were in India, I am quite sure Dunia's dancing ability improved exponentially, as did her flirting with the guards. If she did iron at all, each stroke would have glided to the Bollywood beat. In truth, however, I don't believe she ever bothered to work at the house in Taimani – although she may well have visited to get some respite from her family.

When I returned, the door creaked open, like in those old-fashioned movies, and I entered a dustbowl. It was a house of horrors and I turned into a witch. The electricity didn't work, the gas for the bukhari had run out and the credit on my phone had finished – which was exactly the way I felt. It was freezing, late at night, I was miserable and a layer of thick dust covered everything.

Early the next day, when I had calmed down a little, I spoke to Gracie. I told her I was at the end of my tether and that I couldn't stand it any more. Although I had always felt torn, not wanting Dunia's family's demise on my conscience, my beliefs now lay crumpled in the corner, along with the unironed laundry.

Gracie is a powerful mediator and could probably bring peace to the Middle East. She can smooth out the most sensitive situations and her wicked sense of humour charms her many friends and colleagues. Her patience and forbearance have undoubtedly preserved our friendship. But this time, even Gracie's renowned negotiating skills floundered in the face of my frustration.

Gracie called Dunia to break the news.

Her work here really was done.

14. The Locationship

REPORT: *TV stations across Afghanistan announce that Mullah Omar was assassinated five days ago.*

PREDICTION: *Intelligence agencies say the situation on the ground will deteriorate quickly.*

CONCLUSION: *False rumour or propaganda.*

REACTION: *OK. Let's party.*

A few people milled about near the round table in the lobby at the Gandamack Lodge waiting to use the loo – the one with the overwhelming stench of the mothballs piled high in the urinal. Someone leafed through the books on display and, as it was a Thursday night, the Afghan vendor had his jewellery and artefacts on display by the front door. A waiter walked by with trays of expensive and mostly inedible food on his way from the kitchen, passing the much larger WC that nobody ever seemed to use. He wondered why that was.

After a brief hiatus, Jesus appeared in the wooden doorway of the narrow washroom. He walked down the dimly lit corridor, with its worn, sunken, black-and-white-tiled floors, turned left, went outside and headed down to the British-themed pub, looking for his girlfriend. He was pissed. Benazir, on the other hand, was pissed off.

'What the hell have you been doing?' she asked.

Jesus was happy to let the noise of the blaring music and the din of the crowd absorb her anger. He decided to ignore any flicker of conflict – that was what he dealt with at work, day in and day out, in the field and now out. He needed a break, not a break-up.

'I bumped into a couple of people before I went to the loo; you know how it is – we were chatting,' he said eventually.

She knew exactly how it was, and her bullshit meter was twitching wildly. He couldn't resist women and she felt she couldn't leave him alone for a second. He didn't really have a type, and seemed to prefer quantity over quality, always concerned about how his past would impact on their future. She knew that, before they'd started their relationship, he had sometimes had sex with one woman at lunch and then taken another out for dinner. He had just turned forty, had never been married, had no history of a sustained relationship, didn't want kids, and loved his foreign missions. For obvious reasons, she wasn't sure if she could ever trust him, and that had led to tremendous friction from the very start. And Benazir knew she had her own issues too.

Picking up the bottle of red wine from the bar, Benazir grabbed two glasses and hauled Jesus to the back of the long room. Not only was she steaming mad at him, this boyfriend of just a few weeks, but her head was about to explode like the IEDs that stupid reporter had been gassing about.

The dark-haired, dark-eyed Al Jazeera correspondent had droned on and on about her adventures, about the Taliban she had met, about the soldiers who wanted to confess to her and who, of course, wanted to get her big, fat ass into bed. She came across as if she were the only bloody war correspondent in the entire frickin' world, and as if Afghanistan were her discovery.

As this tedious woman had downed more whiskies, her voice had got louder and louder, and her bravado had matched that of the macho security dudes who drank at the bar. Most of them, Benazir suspected, were gay, with their tight T-shirts, their bulging muscles, moronic sunglasses and way too much bitch-slapping. Benazir's own mission was to take down the military, an institution she neither liked nor respected. Her idea was to do it one man at a time, but it wasn't going that well.

'You should have heard that woman!'

Jesus caught only bits of what Benazir was saying. 'She's only just come to Kabul,' he told her. 'She's covering for their full-time correspondent who's gone on leave. She harangued Annette last night about her time in Iraq.'

Surprisingly, the red two-seater sofa was empty and the two of them slumped onto its limp, worn, down-at-feather concave cushions that hung almost to the ground. Benazir hoped that both the evening and her mood were turning.

Jesus and Benazir had flirted at the office for almost a year, the tension building and building. Each day they had to see each other – he was her boss – and both fought the chemistry and electricity. Too much was at stake if things didn't work out – professionally, it wouldn't have reflected well on either of them. But temptation had proved too hard to resist. They moved in together and told the Afghans they had got married when they were on leave.

Benazir thought back to that first night they'd kissed under the almond tree. She had worn the coveted bustier top made of real peacock feathers that had been on display in the

184

shop window she passed every day on Qala-e Fatullah Road. It was so outrageous and she had worn it with tight skinny jeans and super-high shoes to one of the infamous summer parties. When they'd left later that evening they were ripped on hash. Of course, she had thought she would be the one to change him . . .

Oh God, wondered Benazir to herself. Why do I do these things? She had planned to write a book called *Why Are Women So Stupid? And Yes, That Means You*. She had wanted them to be one of those rare foreign couples who had both met their perfect partner; she had dreams of leaving with a husband – in this case her second – not a broken heart. She wanted a relationship, not just a locationship . . . But Kabul was a city of sex, drugs and danger, where military contractors, human-rights activists and journalists were commingled, saving Afghans from themselves and their ignorance.

That heady combination supposedly justified everything. You need to have fun to do the job, the mantra went. You need to have sex to do the job. You need to party and drink, so that you can do the job. Puh, what crap, she thought. How had she morphed into a modern-day Missoni-missionary preaching gender equality while making lots of money? And, she suspected, making not much difference?

•••

Benazir parted the curtains with the same sense of drama she applied to most things. As they did almost every day, the crystal beams of sunlight tore through the window. For Benazir and Jesus, the best part of the weekend lay before them, starting with brunch at the new Le Jardin restaurant, then home together. Their routine, as much as they had established one, entailed snuggling up to watch one of the pirate DVDs they had bought at their favourite shop in town. The quiet before the storm.

That day, as he often did, Jesus wondered how it was possible that they could go so easily from insane happiness to sheer madness in virtually a matter of seconds. They could be blissfully happy, and then toxic. How did a romantic morning, a peaceful brunch with friends and a movie have the potential to descend into its own full-blown horror story? 'Instead of watching *Drag Me to Hell*,' he yelled across the room, 'come and shag me to hell.'

Benazir's big brown eyes filled with tears of laughter. And for that minute at least the fighting stopped. But the issues never went away.

She sensed he had forgotten what had brought him out here in the first place and suspected he had lost touch with his mission and his goal. He was here to work, to help create livelihoods and better lives, but he had started to suffer from 'little prince' syndrome, thinking he was the centre of the universe.

He was famous in this little expat world – he and others living out dreams they couldn't fulfil anywhere else, only here in the intensity of Kabul, where war, death and disaster formed the backdrop of everyday life.

Had he been in the field too long? What did too long actually mean? She struggled with the same questions herself. It was one of those interminable debates that they always ended up falling out over. More than falling out. That was the problem: they didn't just fall out; their arguments were bitter and poisonous.

He accused her of being controlling, needy, neurotic and insanely jealous. None of which was untrue – there was a lot of trauma in her past, tragic secrets that she couldn't share, and this did impact on her reactions and her relationship with him. She knew it. But he was no saint either. Jesus found that her ultra-left-wing views, formed by outmoded socialist beliefs, skewed her perspective on things like NGO interaction with the military, which had become a reality. She nicknamed him Jesus because he was so evangelical in his beliefs about the good they were doing in Afghanistan; Benazir had lost her faith in the mission.

But their arguments about this and about being in the country for too long were ultimately academic. At some point all the foreigners would have to leave. Benazir knew that and she knew Jesus wasn't ready, but she had had enough. Seven years in the field meant she no longer had perspective and judgement, and she wasn't sure she cared. That frightened her. On a positive note, though, Jesus had brought an end to her addiction to dodgy Afghan mini-warlords who provided that edge of danger and exoticism she craved.

OXFAM REPORT: *A sixteen-year-old girl, seven months pregnant, was brought into a police station. Her tongue was almost completely severed, and she was so violently beaten that her unborn child died.*

The husband denied charges of homicide and aggravated assault. The police said they could not hold him without evidence.

Stupid bitch. She probably deserved it . . .

The report had come out earlier in the day and it haunted Jesus. Benazir would be devastated, he thought. Luckily, she was attending a conference and wouldn't have heard about it yet.

When Farah called, he overcompensated. 'Don't worry if you can't come in to work today,' he said soothingly to his head of staff. He had a calm demeanour and a deep-rooted desire to help. His French NGO's mandate was to improve women's capacity to earn a livelihood by providing financing for small businesses, and part of the programme entailed explaining their rights according to the constitution. He spoke to Farah about the Oxfam report. She said she had heard about it. It was horrific, she said.

Jesus tempered his conversation and tone accordingly. 'We're so behind in the project,' he said to Farah. 'I need to explain what is going on to head office because they will not give us the rest of the funding if we don't deliver.'

'I'm talking to the women,' she said.

'My bosses think I'm not doing my job, Farah *jan*,' he said, sympathetically. It was all such a muddle.

Farah was well aware of the problem. She had instructed the women on what they had to do, but it was hard for them to work on designs that were so different from anything they could relate to. And they had so many other chores. They had to cook and look after the children, clean the house and cater to the needs of their demanding husbands. Deadlines meant nothing to them. Neither did Christmas or the project that was so far away in the capital. Most of the women had never left the village, never mind the province, and talk of elections and women's rights and high-street stores mystified them.

The project had been doomed from the start. All of them – Farah, Benazir and Jesus – they all knew it. It was a waste of money, like so many projects before it. A French woman had managed to raise millions of dollars, drumming up donations in London, Washington and Paris so that women in Afghanistan could make jewellery to sell to an international market. It was the dream ticket. Supposedly.

The woman was well connected, smart, devoted and fabulous at self-promotion. She had managed to get some of her politically influential friends involved, which opened doors. And to be fair, it was no small achievement to have raised this kind of money. In time and with practice the women might have even been able to make the jewellery with the necessary level of skill, but the problems as the project panned out were proving insurmountable: the camera phones that would allow the women to see the designs they were supposed to copy never arrived from the donors; a satellite company had promised free service, which would enable the women to connect to Kabul, but they had gone bankrupt; poor, uneducated village women were supposed to craft high-end designs for a highly competitive Western market.

Added to all that, the areas in which the women were employed were remote and dangerous and the expats who worked for the NGO, including Jesus, couldn't get there to teach or mentor or undertake any sort of quality control. All that was down to Farah, whose husband had his own misgivings, not least that Afghan women did not travel on their own.

These problems were compounded by the logistical nightmare of transporting the products from the villages, some of which were cut off for months during winter. And once the goods arrived in the capital, the only efficient way to ship anything out of the country was by international courier, which cost a fortune, making the pieces prohibitively expensive.

Even if the system had worked, and the technology and other promises had fallen into place, having to pay off corrupt officials made one of Jesus's colleagues remark that she would rather stick pins in her eyes. At the back of everyone's mind was always the misuse of grant funds. So much had just disappeared into big black holes. Jesus and

Benazir had fought endlessly about the futility of it all.

As the stock for the holiday season could now not be delivered on time, the big stores were cancelling their orders, Jesus told Farah. Even if they were running charities and not businesses, they still had deadlines and commitments.

Farah stalled. She knew the women they employed were good women, and they enjoyed the slight independence this small amount of money gave them. The work also offered them a little bit of self-esteem. But the Western rules of work simply didn't make sense to them.

'They are doing the best they can,' she said to Jesus, but in reality she knew it was another lost project just like all the others. It was always the same theatrics – in which governments were able to show they were using their foreign aid budgets, where foreigners felt they were helping people who needed help, where everyone was making money (some more than others), and all with nothing sustainable at the end. And what was the point? The troops were pulling out and the aid money was drying up.

Heroin was an easier option.

As if there weren't enough complications in day-to-day life, there was always temptation, Benazir found. And too much temptation was hard to resist.

Benazir had masses of fabulous, rope-like dark hair (her best feature, as far as she was concerned), a more Nutella than hazelnut complexion, and deep, dark eyes. She looked like the women painted on the sides of Pakistani trucks, and men wanted to bury themselves in her flesh. Her name was really Shahnaz. She got her nickname from the way she wore her hijab, right at the very back of her head, like Pakistan's murdered Prime Minister Bhutto.

Afghanistan had attracted Benazir like a magnet. She liked the chaos. She liked to be around it, to create it, feed on it, tread its thin borderline with death. Everyone craved the drama; it made them feel wanted and alive. Not surprising, then, that when a Frenchman had offered her a double vodka at L'Atmosphère, Benazir had said '*Merci*' with a sly smile and downed it in one, even though it was early afternoon.

The Frenchman admired her spirit, and pulling out a cigarette, he asked, 'Drive?'

In five minutes they were at his house. In five minutes and thirty seconds, they were in his bed. By five o'clock it was time for Benazir to go home.

The bomb exploded at Finest, the Wazir Akbar Khan branch of the supermarket chain, on 28 January 2011.

The shop stood on a busy road near a busy roundabout, not far from many embassies. Foreigners and rich Afghans enjoyed the store's selection of imported goods. It wasn't exactly Fortnum's, but if you needed Oreos you could find them there.

Benazir had a good view from her apartment of the store's large white-and-green sign, the two saplings, and the silver cars parked outside.

The noise. At first she thought it was simulated explosions; she heard those all the time. But it was louder and the air was different. She sped to the window only to see the devastation below. People – crowds of injured people. People screaming, wailing, weeping, bodies, blood. Journalists. Cars and traffic.

Smoke and fire erupted inside. Products flew around the shop, debris scattering onto the outside steps. A woman in a red scarf, hair up, blood pouring down her face, was led away. Eight people lay dead inside; more were injured.

A bearded man in sunglasses carried a young girl wearing running shoes.

A child wrapped in posters carried out. Dead.

More dead were brought out. An Afghan family of six – mother, father, four children – they had been standing next to the suicide bomber when he detonated his vest. A doctor and a lawyer, prominent activists. Afghanistan's future.

The Taliban claimed responsibility.

Incidents like this brought reality home. Most of the time you could forget about it; on the ground, everyday life seemed – and was – more normal than when viewed from abroad, where bombs, beheadings and political turmoil painted an incredibly bleak picture. Every year the parameters of normality were concertinaed, yet, paradoxically, the city was safe.

Until it wasn't. Until a suicide bomber exploded and ruined lives. Then the sense of security was shaken, and everyone remembered they lived their lives in the shadow of grim chance.

The fire trucks and ambulances arrived.

Jesus rushed home. Benazir fell weeping into his arms.

In the end, Benazir and Jesus found themselves hurling insults as corrosive as acid. It was the last straw.

Benazir called to say goodbye from the airport. 'I'm sorry,' she said to Jesus. People were already lining up to board.

'It's better this way,' Jesus replied, glad that she was going. 'But you actually didn't have to leave if you believed in the mission.'

'We're different,' Benazir said, reflecting. 'I couldn't stand it. We played right into the hands of the conservatives.

This is exactly the Western decadence that the Taliban preach against. The sex, the parties, the drinking – everything this country is fighting against, we've shoved right in their faces and they don't feel that they can protect their society from us.'

'The world has changed,' he told her. 'Afghans want change, the young generation especially.'

'I'm not so sure that's true, but even if it is, I couldn't live in our isolated and constructed world. It didn't feel right. And do you know what the worst thing is?' asked Benazir.

'Tell me,' said Jesus, calm and, for the last time, sympathetic.

'We brought them this dream of freedom, and then we kept them out. We abandoned them to their fate while we partied on.'

15. Where the Hell is Zaman?

June 2012

Dear Heidi

I know you have not heard from me for some time. I am sorry not to have been in touch, but there is a very good reason. I was kidnapped.

You know my work takes me to all sorts of insecure places in order to assess the security situation. I have pretty good contacts, which is why my information is much valued.

My focus this time was to look at how the Taliban made their money in one of the remote valleys, and in Wardak and Logar provinces, which included money laundering by high-ranking officials.

I had already received warnings to stop my inquiries, but that is not my way. I met one of the VIPs in the Taliban regime who was involved in kidnapping six UNAMA election staff in 2005. At the end of our meeting, he told me to give some of my friends his number in case anything happened to me. I did this, and returned to the valley to meet someone who'd promised to take me to Pakistan for an interview with a big-gun in the Peshawar shura.

An hour later I was hooded and handcuffed, and kept in a distress position for twenty-four hours.

Following that ordeal a number of my good hosts visited me - beating me and torturing me; three times with electric shocks. Nothing too serious! Most of the time I spent relaxing in a cage, sometimes for up to three days at a time, and every day I was hooded like a falcon for up to five hours. I still cannot fly, however.

Then something too strange happened. They asked me to help them update their BlackBerry Messenger and their Windows systems. I know this must make you proud as you are Canadian.

They started talking to me more gently after that, which is when they laid out their conditions for my release. These were:

1. I should not write anything about politics.

2. I should not work on any project related to the Taliban.

3. I should not stay active politically or socially, which includes not giving speeches in mosques or other places.

I am alive because that VIP asked them to not kill me. Otherwise, they wouldn't care and I have little doubt they would have ended my life. They may still do this if I don't keep my word; and then my family would also be in danger.

So now I am silent.

    Yours,

    Zaman

16. The Karen Woo Story

Karen had a long, oval face, a brittle thinness, an elfin charm and an ability to make friends easily. She also liked a man who could dig a trench.

No doubt our paths would have eventually crossed in the small Kabul village, but as it happened, Caroline Richards, wife of the former head of the UK military, put us together. That was typical. Karen seemed to know everybody.

We were introduced originally because Karen wanted to ship medical supplies from the UK to Afghanistan, and as it happened I knew just the man who could help – someone who had supplied the North Koreans with prescription drugs.

Karen arrived in the capital shortly after I did, and rather than have the regulation introductory coffee I suggested yoga, hosted at the Norwegian embassy, always a popular event packed with people – some familiar, others not.

As it turned out, Benazir was also at the class. She had met Karen – Dr Woo – in her previous incarnation when Karen worked at RMSI, a company that carried out medical evacuations and provided medical services to the expat community. Karen had been Benazir's doctor and they had become friends. At the end of the class we all hopped into Benazir's waiting taxi and headed home with the last rays of the day's sunlight fading.

It was difficult to imagine Karen quitting school at sixteen to become a professional dancer and, oddly, a wing walker, though that, it seemed, was the case. Twenty years later she had moved to Kabul, a general surgeon disillusioned with the NHS, engaged to a man she had met a few months earlier and en route to a big medical adventure in the north of the country.

She did dance incredibly well. Together with Jenner and her fiancé Paddy Smith, a former soldier turned security consultant, we went to the Relax guesthouse – another location for yet another legendary summer party. The compound spread out over acres of green grass. There was an air of languidness about both the evening and Karen's dancing. A sense of old-world decadence hung in the atmosphere; there was a feeling of completeness, of men and women in their prime, of the world outside being distant and foreign and yet integral. Intensity rose from the very soil. Situation and place distinguished the otherwise ordinary scene. People drank in clusters, some sprawled in a corner inside, near the indoor bar, while others danced. Karen stood out as she moved seductively.

Beer in hand, Paddy watched the woman to whom he would be married in a few weeks. He had lived, worked and partied in Kabul for years and years and finally he had met the love of his life. There weren't many of those stories, but enough exceptional and meaningful couples to give many hope. Karen and Paddy were one of them.

Karen's speciality was maternal and neonatal care. She was on her way to Nooristan to bring much-needed health services to the population there. The team would be led by two very experienced men, Dan Terry and Tom Little, who had lived and worked in Afghanistan for decades; they spoke the language, had travelled the country, raised their children there and knew the people – they were respected and invited and protected. Karen would be in safe hands.

Few people travelled to Nooristan in those days, and it sounded like a fabulous adventure, a great story in the making. I was tempted to see if there was an opportunity for me. There wasn't, but even if there had been Jenner would have talked me out of it. I admired people like Karen and her colleagues who could provide essential medical care for communities that needed it.

The trek to this remote northern province was going to be both a physically arduous and an expensive venture. To help Karen on her way, a handful of expats had organized an event at the Kabul Health Club to raise money for the expedition.

The club had recently been taken over and renovated by a young Afghan-American couple. They hoped to turn the space into a sanctuary where foreigners and Afghans alike would come to exercise, meet, eat and work. The large garden alone had received a US$25,000 facelift.

That night, groups of people sat on big, bed-like structures arranged in a semicircle. Quite a number had turned out in support of the event. As one of the main organizers, Jenner had volunteered his bartending services. After the speeches, the videos and the buffet, Karen's place on the expedition was almost secured.

Days after her return, she would fly back to the UK to marry Paddy at the Chelsea registry office. Clearly excited about their upcoming wedding, the couple planned to have Woo-Smith cubs as soon as possible; they already had three surrogate plastic parrots, after all.

•••

Jenner, Karen and I met frequently, especially at the Flower Street Café. I hadn't known Karen long, but in the course of our many meetings during our relatively brief friendship, one of the things we talked about a lot was her wedding. She couldn't wait to marry Paddy.

Of the many conversations from that time, there are few that I remember in detail, but one stands out – even then it seemed so very unsettling that I immediately dismissed it. Karen was in the midst of the massive preparations for her trek. She was confident about going, and so determined, and had never confided any doubts to me. So when we talked about the wedding in London, I was shocked when she casually threw the words 'If I come back alive' into a sentence about plans and parties. I told her not to be so ridiculous. My response might have had more to do with my own fear of death than an accurate appraisal of the situation.

Not long before her departure Karen and I headed to Mandai market by the river, an old multistorey maze of at least 600 small, tightly packed, family-owned shops and stalls selling fabrics and dresses. Karen took to Afghan dress much more readily than I did, and ended up buying a number of shalwar kameez, but no wedding dress. She had something else in mind, she explained, and a tailor was in the process of creating it for her.

I arranged a dinner party for Karen at my Taimani house. Other Heidi, now working for the State Department and based at the American embassy, was there, and she brought with her Jungle Ben Hart. He came bearing chocolates and wine, and poured on his thick Southern charm to great effect. In the course of the evening, Karen received the good news that the last bit of her funding had come through. She was on her way.

The day finally arrived and Karen and the rest of her group set off. Paddy and Karen were in constant phone and text contact throughout the trip. We'd all check in with Paddy to get updates, and he continued to party, waiting for her return and their wedding.

The trek was indeed gruelling, over harsh but beautiful landscape. Karen kept a video diary and the team attended to the villagers who came from miles away to receive the only medical attention they'd had access to for years.

As the trip wound down, Karen and the others safely crossed the provincial border from Nooristan into Badakhshan, the rugged province in the north-east part of the country that shares a border with Pakistan and Tajikistan. They were on the home stretch.

During the trip Karen continued to prepare for her wedding, writing the vows she planned to make to Paddy just days later. She read them to him:

I love you for the person you are.

I accept your strengths and your weaknesses equally.

I hope as a team we will share many happy times.

May our life together always be blessed.

They said goodbye.

Then silence.

Something was wrong. Paddy couldn't raise Karen by phone, and she hadn't responded to any text messages. He topped up the credit on her satellite phone, just in case. Still nothing. And no communication from anyone else on the team.

Panic set in.

Hours passed. And more hours . . .

Jenner had told me, and Karen – in fact, anyone who would listen – not to trek there. He thought they should helicopter in, do what they needed to do and head out after a few hours. The terrain was dangerous, he said.

'Trekking will alert the entire valley,' he argued. 'What's the point? There are too many insurgents near that border with Pakistan, too many thieves, too many variables, too many unknowns.'

He'd said this to Karen on many occasions, he'd told me almost incessantly and had also mentioned it to a mutual friend who'd said, 'I can't tell her not to go. That would be like clipping the wings of a beautiful butterfly.' Not what Jenner wanted to hear.

It was early in August 2010 when I dropped by to see Gracie at her office. She was waiting for me at the top of the wide staircase.

Looking back, I remember it was as if there were an unexplained heaviness in the air. Only in retrospect was that apparent.

'*Hola*,' I said, pretty chirpily from the dark hallway.

I did not get a chirpy greeting in return.

'I have to tell you something,' said Gracie, and I followed her into a dark, empty office. How oddly she was acting, I thought, unable to decipher her behaviour. As she was so solemn I thought perhaps she had been fired. If that wasn't the case, maybe something had happened at home, in Sydney. Was her son OK? And I knew her mother hadn't been well . . .

'Karen was executed.'

People say the words, you hear them, you know what they mean, but they don't make sense.

It didn't seem possible.

The bodies were found beside their bullet-ridden vehicles, she told me. The ambush was the worst attack on aid workers in the region in thirty years.

'Are you OK?' she asked, tears welling up in her eyes.

I thought of Karen's words: 'If I come back alive . . . '

I immediately called Paddy. I couldn't imagine the shock. It was too much to process.

Paddy said she'd been shot twice in the back. She'd died instantly. It was little comfort.

At first the Taliban claimed responsibility. Rumours spread that the team – Karen and nine of her eleven colleagues – were murdered because they were spies, carried bibles and were proselytizing; but their humanitarian work had been well received by Afghans, who worried that after this attack no one would return to help them.

We – Jenner and I – saw Paddy before he went to see Karen for the last time. He was going to kiss her goodbye. Then he would take her body back to London.

It was just nine months since Karen and Paddy had met and fallen in love.

Karen, young, attractive, a doctor, became the media story in the predictable way. Others didn't capture the imagination as she did, and in the UK it made media sense: she was British. There were six Americans, one German and two Afghans, one of whom survived because he recited verses from the Koran; the other had left days before.

Karen's death was no more tragic than the others', of course, even if hers was a sexy story for the media to tell. When Paddy gave me the first interview, which was published in the *Mail on Sunday*, I tried hard to emphasize that. Functioning on automatic and alcohol, Paddy said that in his heart he was married to her. He wore Karen's wedding ring on a piece of string around his neck. We all wanted to cry.

As the days passed, and I had to write more on Karen's death, I struggled with my anger. I was angry that she had taken the risk, not listening to Jenner and to the many others who had given the same advice, even at the Kabul Health Club event. I was angry that she was dead. I was angry that she wasn't coming back. And I was angry that she wouldn't now be able to help the many Afghans who needed her. Really angry. And very, very sad.

The media turned Karen into a heroine – but that's not who she was. She was like all the others who had devoted their time, their careers and their hearts to a bewitching country and its people. She wasn't a saint; there was a darkness there too and a restlessness that many of us shared. But she was one of the unlucky ones who just never returned.

17. Frontier Dispatches

Kabul Diary, June 2012
Monday

I have already overstayed by several weeks my planned journey of only a few days, sucked into the Kabul vortex. Despite the fact that it's a war zone and talk is of the country going to hell in a handcart, life is good.

It's probably really good for those who are laundering money, and a lot of that goes on. My flight from Dubai is full of men wearing piran tomban, and oddly all carrying matching briefcases. They could have attended the same conference, but I suspect they are returning having deposited cash in the emirate, where so much of the wonga goes.

Tonight I am invited to dinner. My host is a member of the former royal family, an oaf of a man with unflattering aristocratic pretensions. All over the walls of his house are pictures of Afghans from decades and centuries ago.

17. FRONTIER DISPATCHES

'Who are they?' I ask.

Kings, prime ministers, more kings and princes, he says.

Unfortunately, all men with moustaches look the same. I must take better care to vet the people I hang out with.

A sinewy French woman with the harsh potato-eater features of a Van Gogh peasant gives massages in another room. By the time it's my turn, she's too tired. She teaches street children circus skills.

I am actually here to work, something I try to slip into my very active social life.

Over many years I have written for the UK's *Mail On Sunday*. I happened to be living in Dubai when I got a call from them saying that a British woman had been kidnapped. The paper asked me to go to Kabul as soon as possible. I needed a visa – easy to get at that time – and arrived the next day.

Of the story this is what I know so far: in the Faizabad office where Helen Johnston and her Medair colleagues work, there is a wonderful view on to the rough and wild river. The two-storey house stands on the long and wide main road in the provincial capital of Badakhshan, and has a verandah in the front. Take the recently paved highway and you will be in China. This is the ancient Silk Road. In many parts of this remote Afghan area, things have not changed for hundreds of years.

The terrain is so rough and villages so isolated that the only way to reach them is on horseback, and as the sun was setting Helen Johnston and her three colleagues rode to the isolated villages where they work – Yawan, Raghistan and Kohistan. At the top of a mountain, this time three armed men appeared in front of them on the path, and one pointed a gun.

Tuesday

The Kabul social scene moves at a hectic pace. Tonight there is a screening of a film, *Reel Unreel*, at the bombed-out cinema called Behzad, in the old city. What an astonishing place. The peeling paint is from decades ago and an ugly, faded, hospital green. There is exposed brick and craters in the concrete. Red fold-up lawn chairs are set up under the open air (the roof having collapsed long ago) in front of a large screen. This is one of the most extraordinary events I have been to.

An Afghan-Swiss photojournalist snaps pictures for the *New Yorker*, policemen in Clouseau-like uniforms watch as locals – women in burqas and children – as well as expats gather.

I catch the tail end of the movie, which doesn't get great reviews. It runs for just over twenty minutes and is about a boy rolling an old metal film reel through the streets of Kabul. Dinner after is held at the Queen's Palace, meticulously restored by the Aga Khan Foundation. Lanterns hang from trees and people sit on large Afghan rugs ringed by large cushions known as *toshaks*. It is quite exquisite.

Afghan food is served. Usually it is heavy and swimming in oil, but tonight it is not only delicious but the orange rice is delicate and lightly fragrant. It is a small gathering during which I talk to Zolay, still tiny, still trilingual, still designing the same things and still lovely. I still hate the clothes.

Medair, a small Christian organization, worked among Salafis, radical Islamists. In its lemon-coloured offices this did not seem to cause problems. As one Afghan remarked, 'It has taken fourteen hundred years and we are not yet real Muslims, so how can a few bibles convert us to Christianity? We're not afraid.'

My friend Zaman helps me identify the Afghan men who were kidnapped and finds out as much information as he can for me. We arrange to interview them by phone. Zaman speaks to them and provides me with some great information about where and how they were held, what happened during that time. He has a fairly good idea who the kidnappers are. The released men are anxious, worried and still recovering from their ordeal. Zaman has excellent sources and deep knowledge, which he freely shares. His life has been spent traversing the country. It is pure serendipity that we met, through another *Afghanista* friend helping me with the story. The ability to make incredible contacts has always been one of the great bonuses and necessities of journalism.

Ironic that a few months later Zaman found himself in the same hostage situation.

Wednesday

dOCUMENTA (13) comes to Kabul. It is the first time that this prestigious international contemporary art project has been held in a war zone.

Established in 1955, it takes place every five years in Kassel, Germany (as well as Banff and Cairo/Alexandria). It has been brought to Afghanistan by the Goethe-Institut, and they have chosen the Queen's Palace for the exhibition, an astonishing location, with views over the mountains that form a daisy chain around the capital. Five international Afghan artists were selected in the process, which began two and a half years ago.

Zolaykha Sherzad has made an oversized chapan, the coat that Karzai wears. Zalmai, the Afghan-Swiss photographer, photographs transformed weapons of war.

That night, like every night, the lights across Kabul illuminate the mountains surrounding the city. Certainly, this is progress. But the electricity comes from Tajikistan and Uzbekistan. 'They can just switch it off any time they like,' says a friend.

A helicopter lands on top of a steep, treeless mountain in Badakhshan. The valley is silent. Fifteen minutes later a second helicopter lands. Nearby, two more hover overhead, ready to provide air cover. The SAS prepare for the rescue of Helen Johnston and the others.

Thursday

My new friend Habib, whom I met at dOCUMENTA, picks me up in his 1966 Russian Volga, and takes me to a school where thousands of children go every day, studying in two-hour shifts. He wants to show me the appalling condition it's in. What he is most incensed about is the toilets. They stink. They stink because there is no money to take away the waste. They cannot afford toilet paper. There is no water.

Kids wipe their hands on the walls. It does not bear thinking about.

As we talk, a boy of about sixteen makes a rude hand gesture to my female American friend who has joined us on this mission. She is now furious and tells Habib and the acting principal, who is with us.

They catch up to the boy and reprimand him. 'This is what is wrong with Afghanistan,' she says. 'They have no respect for women. Nothing will change if this continues.'

She talks to another boy, who complains that there is no discipline in the school, and she says he must set an example. She asks, 'Why do you boys do that? You have mothers and sisters and cousins.' He looks sheepish.

A few hundred dollars would fix the bathroom situation for six months, but more would be needed to put glass in the windows. People on an individual basis want to help, but no one is interested in changing the system – not USAID, which funds many projects, or the Ministry of Health or Education. Too complicated. Short-term is better than long-term, like Orwell's four legs are better than two.

I tell Habib that I will do my best to write about this.

Under cover of darkness the SAS mobilize. By the time the rescue ends, five Afghan guards lie dead, including Commander Mahajer, the former Hezb-i-Islami member who had masterminded the kidnap.

Workers know that almost 100 per cent of the danger doesn't come from the villages, where communities protect them, but on the journeys to and from them. Badakhshan is the same province where Karen Woo was killed. They were luckier than Karen and her group.

Friday

It's the weekend and brunch is the main activity on a Friday. In the spring and summer, what better way to spend it than outside eating at Le Jardin, which has recently opened its very large premises and vast garden. By this time we all know that the troops will be pulling out, that the numbers in the international community will shrink, and that the vast amounts of floating cash will dry up. Opening a restaurant of such colossal proportions doesn't make any sense to me, nor does the continued building of vast mansions which people hope to rent out at inflated prices to NGOs and the like. Never mind. I order salade niçoise, although the Afghans I am with don't trust the cleanliness of the salad leaves, and they go for omelettes. Someone orders a giant raspberry-coloured macaroon with vanilla ice cream. A little chewy, but remarkable all the same.

Later, we call a jeweller who comes to the restaurant with his rings and things. Mafias control the lapis and emerald mines, and it is actually cheaper to buy Afghan stones in London than in Kabul as they are smuggled out.

The jewellery is very nice and a frenzy of consumption begins.

The Taliban were never able to take over Badakhshan, but now mullahs educated in Pakistani madrassas return with much more fundamental views and preach against foreigners, saying they are spies. What have foreigners brought but war, they ask.

Zaman has opened a café in Faizabad and wants to start a debating society – we are looking for people who could participate.

Saturday

A case of beer now costs US$140. It's getting more and more difficult to source. The dealer who delivers the alcohol, at some risk, has so many people to pay off. He leaves my friend an enormous chunk of hash, although my friend doesn't smoke, and stays to watch TV with a group of us for a while. He is getting married on Monday, although he wasn't even engaged a few weeks ago. Tajik vodka is readily available, if you are brave enough to try it. The shop at the corner sells it.

Speaking of marriage, I use Trust taxis to get around the city. There are a number of car services that cater to foreigners. They know where everyone lives, know the gossip, and can tell you who goes where.

The drivers speak English, and are great. One conversation is about the pull-out. There is anxiety about the future. Where will money and jobs come from? We get on to this topic talking about weddings. Karzai has banned big weddings due to the outrageous expense, but no one seems to take any notice. The figures are mind-boggling. It's not unusual for these affairs – deadly dull by all accounts – to cost US$30,000. That includes renting the wedding hall, food, inviting everyone you have ever known and spending literally thousands of dollars on gold jewellery for the bride. People are in debt for years.

During the kidnap Helen Johnston had apparently kept very calm and was said to be strong and unafraid. Most of the time in captivity the four hostages remained silent.

Sunday

It is difficult to convey how extraordinary life is for those of us privileged to be in Kabul at this time. I imagine Saigon at the end of the 1950s, when the French left Indochina, when colonialism and communism clashed, must have had a similar atmosphere.

In 2012 Kabul restaurants aren't quite as busy as they once were, the big projects supported by institutions like USAID are losing their funding, people are leaving, heading for the next big story. The large poppy palaces that have mushroomed over the past several years, built in a Pakistani style, have For Rent signs stuck up.

House prices are down significantly from even last year. A friend is selling an old family house that he has restored. He has had to pay a US$16,000 bribe in order to process the sale. If he hadn't, he was told he would have to wait two years before the sale would be allowed to go through.

Security in Kabul is reasonable. Things are fine until they aren't, but the mood is fairly gloomy. Again it reminds me of Vietnam, but another era, more like the fall of Saigon in 1975, when everyone was waiting for that last chopper flight out before the city went dark.

Helen Johnston did not give us an interview.

18. Lara Croft of the Kabubble

Sunlight periscoped through the squat doorway, illuminating the tall, thin figure with the slicked-back blonde hair scraped into a ponytail.

Lara Croft stood, legs shoulder-width apart, with guns and ammo spread all about her. She knocked back whisky after whisky, while her minions worked on a getaway plan.

I walked down the concrete steps of the German guesthouse and into this comic-strip world. It was not quite noon.

Debbie looked pale, dazed and traumatized. Normally the life and soul of the Kabubble party, she had just fled her Afghan husband. Grave threats had been made. She needed to get out of the country fast, and Lara Croft – aka Vivienne, an Australian who worked for a security firm – was on the case, procuring flights, safe houses and other logistical essentials. She seemed totally insane.

My assigned role was to get us a room at the Serena. Afghanistan's only five-star hotel had five-star security.

There was an X-ray machine at the door, guards from the Ministry of Interior and a no-gun policy. When Vivienne arrived with Debbie, the first thing she did was toss her weapons on the bed. So much for tight security.

That evening we ordered pizza, and Debbie cried about abandoning her life of the past six years, in which she had built up two businesses and made a home. This American hairdresser had come to Kabul to help Afghan women, and had set up a beauty school and a salon; she was considerably less upset about dumping her husband, who already had a wife and eight children in Saudi Arabia.

I did not feel at all prepared for such an alarming situation. In places like Kabul, people are supposed to have grab bags full of cash and clothes stationed by the front door, ready to go should they need to be evacuated at a moment's notice. I did once have a grab bag with a change of clothes, some medication – probably Cipro – sunscreen, emergency food bars and water. But as the weeks went by, the clothes got worn, the bars got eaten, the water snatched as I left the house, and the sunscreen was applied at the mirror by the front door. The cash got spent on domestic bills and emergency Chicken Street shopping, important for keeping the Afghan economy afloat. You never think it's going to happen to you.

I half expected Vivienne to abseil through the window

the next morning but, more prosaically, she knocked on the door, laden with Afghan disguises for Debbie's covert escape.

With Debbie safely evacuated, it now turned out I was being threatened too. Was the danger real? I wasn't courageous enough to find out. For my protection, Vivienne took me to her villa. There we found a slumbering, pickled body of a man with grey hair flopped on the bed. Next to him was an AK-47. Seemingly oblivious to me, Vivienne lay down beside the man and cuddled up to his AK-47. This was her boyfriend, it turned out. Thirty-odd years old, but his hard-drinking, hard-partying Kabul life had aged him prematurely.

Alcohol fuelled a lot in Afghanistan, including this relationship, and the couple's virtually incoherent conversations were all about guns and bullets. While I was glad Debbie was out of harm's way, I had mixed feelings about entrusting my own safety to this woman. But I had been staying with Debbie up until now, and the great escape had left me essentially homeless. Moving house in Afghanistan was logistically challenging, and I hadn't really got my head around what I was going to do. I needed a few days to take stock and process the possibilities.

I wasn't going to get them. Rumours had erupted on the intelligence grapevine that men were circling Vivienne's house looking for me – who knew why? I had to move again.

I took temporary refuge with my French colleague. She had a beautiful house where she often entertained – seemingly always dressed in leather trousers. One of her housemates was away on a job and she said I could rent his room. The house was located on what was known as Garbage Street, so named for its ever-present piles of rubbish, although these were hardly unique in the capital. While the rest of the house had been decorated with great style and lots of Afghan furniture and artefacts, the room I was given had nothing but a bed and a rucksack in the corner.

At last I felt safe, but in fact the real danger had only just caught up with me. Within twenty-four hours I was incredibly sick – a victim of the kind of germ warfare that makes it impossible to get out of bed. For days I could barely open my eyes. Through a fog of delirium one night I seemed to hear a high-pitched wailing. I thought I had dreamed this, but as the microbes exited my body and I started to recover, I continued to hear that sound. I tried to figure out what it was, and when I was able to stand, I walked over to the corner of the room to find a cat had given birth behind the rucksack.

I was alive – and so were a large number of very cute kittens.

19. Hairdressing in Helmand

In a tiny room at the front of a private house in Lashkar Gah, capital of Helmand province, is one of the city's beauty salons. This is where Royah and her sister Rosiah have been doing women's hair for many years. It is a skill they learned from their mother, Anissah, who in turn was taught by an American three decades ago. The salon doesn't have a name, but is known informally as the beauty salon of Anissah Jan. The room has shiny posters of women with updos that have been preserved in time like aspic, styles both elaborate and old-fashioned, but popular with women who hide behind veils.

Underneath the emerald-green-and-gold cloth covering her like a burqa is Sakinah, the eighteen-year-old bride-to-be. Excited and nervous, she is too shy to be seen by the men who have come into the cramped beauty salon, usually the exclusive preserve of women. The men – one a translator, the other an American diplomat – are here with me. Of the ten women in the room, I am the only one without a headscarf, which is difficult to fit under a helmet. As an embed, I also have to wear a flak jacket.

Sakinah is going to be married later today and her dark hair is wrapped up in rollers in preparation for the sophisticated hairstyle that Royah will create. Her make-up is also resplendent, like the cloth that covers her – heavy and colourful against the desert background in one of the country's most conservative provinces. If you ask me, I say, she looks like a drag queen, but Gracie reprimands me. The Afghans haven't caught on to the more natural look yet, and certainly not for weddings.

On a table in front of the bride sits the palette of brightly coloured eye make-up Royah has been using – grass green, deep-sea blue. Sakinah will be presented to her husband gift-wrapped. 'The brides', explains Royah, 'bring in their own pictures of how they want to look', but most of the time she will create a style to suit the person. 'Just like in Canada,' she says.

The original plan was for Royah to do my hair, but the security situation remains so tense that we only have a few minutes before we will have to leave. Instead, she sits me down in another chair and drags a flat plastic brush through my hair, which is thickened with sand and dust. It usually takes an hour and a half to do bridal hair; I get less than two minutes. The price depends on how much you can afford. Sakinah will pay 500Afs (about US$10) to be made up, but the cost never exceeds 1,500Afs.

Like all good salons everywhere, this place is often the best source of gossip. Royah and her sister have been working out of their house for ten years, and they want to encourage other women to do the same. They worked under the Taliban, but the salon (as opposed to saloon, as it is so often written in these parts) was hidden.

One of the clients at the salon is Fowzea Olomi, director of women's affairs, whom I have just interviewed in her cold, spartan office. Like so many Afghan women she is talkative and forthright, strong and buoyant, not meek and mild. Formerly a teacher and principal who taught Royah's mother, she chastises me when I say that we think women in Helmand cannot leave their houses. 'You are absolutely wrong,' she says.

Despite the fact that winter has come to Afghanistan, Olomi is wearing open-toed shoes without socks. She has her little granddaughter in tow.

Olomi studied science at Kabul University and returned to Helmand to work. Under the Taliban regime the school of which she was principal was closed, but 'Was I supposed to sit quietly?' she asks. 'Ask anyone in Lashkar Gah, they know me because I am a teacher,' she says proudly. 'Three hundred students came to my home and I taught them.'

Surprisingly, she also taught three high-ranking Talib families, including that of the governor. 'They came looking for a teacher for their women and children, girls and boys. They never saw my face and I never saw the faces of the men, but the governor's daughter used to come to my house. I would teach them the holy Koran, writing and reading, tailoring and cooking, and the children wanted to learn English, so I taught them their ABCs. They used to respect teachers.'

The annual budget only covers the salaries for the staff, fuel for cars, and – if they are lucky – stationery. The ministry received financial assistance from non-governmental organizations and the Provincial Reconstruction Team, the NATO-led reconstruction effort first established in Afghanistan in 2001.

Lashkar Gah is considered 'a bubble of modernity' by some, but only in comparison to the districts surrounding it. These are even more conservative. The situation for women is not straightforward by a long chalk. It depends on class, education and so much else. 'If a woman gets sick here, she can go to a male doctor; in the faraway districts it is a tough culture – they have no female doctors, so if a woman is sick, there is not much she can do.'

Hmmm.

In their programmes the PRT have taught women the best way to clean their homes (it is always either dusty or muddy and poor hygiene is a common problem), as well as the concept of composting – so instead of buying vegetables they can grow and sell them. They also teach women about child nutrition – Afghanistan used to have the highest infant mortality rate in the world, and many children are still malnourished. And most importantly, she says, they advise them against using drugs. Helmand is Poppy Central. Recently a women's rights union was launched, but the issues regarding women are still complex.

When the Americans came to Helmand in the 1950s, among other things they built the school Olomi attended. 'Of course, there were American teachers who taught us English and physics. My old English teacher came back two years ago. We forget that Americans helped us a lot. There were lots of doctors and nurses and teachers. Look at the girls' high-school building,' she says. 'It's still working and in good condition thirty years later.' She contrasts it with the building where her department is based: 'There is so much corruption here that after a few years this new building needs refurbishment as it was so badly done. The concrete floor has already been redone two or three times.'

My next stop is Musqa Radio. The country's first all-female radio station, it was set up by Sabawoon Radio, which was originally launched in 2003 with USAID funding. 'There have been lots of changes in the media over these six years,' says Mirwais Pasoon, the Sabawoon Group director and a former journalist. Before, the idea of an independent media didn't exist. 'My aim in setting up Musqa Radio was to provide an opportunity for women to work and talk about things relevant to them.'

In the main radio station, Sabawoon, men and women journalists sit side by side. Previously, there were stories that Sabawoon couldn't cover because men could not go into houses where there were women. 'Having female journalists means we can speak to the women,' explains Pasoon. He hopes that the status quo in Afghanistan will change and that equal rights for women will come about.

The recording studio is a room beside the main station, which has a small transmission box. When the power goes off (as it does when I am there) work stops. Outside, two small pairs of shoes have been left by the door, and their owners – they are teenagers – walk barefoot. Razia, one of Musqa Radio's employees, is tiny. Dressed in a long brownish-coloured coat and matching pants, her head is covered, and she blushes when I ask if she would talk more openly about women's issues, whatever that encompasses, if there were no men present. She says no, but I am quite sure that isn't the case.

She has been working at the station for almost four months, although she trained as a nurse. Her previous job was in the emergency unit of the hospital, and she loved it. Her family, however, were not happy and insisted on her leaving. Nevertheless, her training comes in handy because Musqa puts out programmes about healthcare for women, as well as cooking shows and live interviews on radio about women's problems – like domestic violence, which is rife.

I ask Razia why she likes journalism. 'Because we are connecting to the listeners,' she tells me. Then she apologizes: she has to go back inside. She sits with her colleague Maria, a charismatic girl with a huge smile. They are about to broadcast a poem, a reader's request.

Driving back, I look to see how many women are walking on the streets, and I count very few. All those I do see wear burqas. I notice one mint green one as opposed to the usual blue.

•••

When I return to Kabul a few days later I speak to a female accountant. She is Afghan-born and has never lived anywhere else. She controls the large budget of a private British company. On the day that I meet her she seems concerned. One of the local staff has quit because he doesn't like the fact that she is in a position of power. He has told her to be worried, and she is.

'Afghan men don't like it. They don't like it that I can say no to them if they ask for money. They want women to stay at home. It is very difficult. But we have no problem with foreign men. I know women who trained as lawyers and they just sit at home because of the attitude of men. It is very difficult for women.'

When she was at university another student told her he loved her and she told him she wasn't interested and asked him to leave her alone. Still he persisted. One day he turned up at her house and threw a stone through the window. She and her mother could say nothing without it escalating out of control. 'That man later stabbed someone, and a senior figure in the present government helped him escape,' she tells me.

The story stays the same.

20. Last Days of the Raj

The Taverna was never a good place to go if you were on a diet. You might try to order a salad or tabouleh, but Kamal would override your protestations and dreams of size-zero jeans and send over endless dishes, starting with chicken soup, then fatayer and kibbe and many of the other delicious Lebanese specialities that his restaurant served. Finally, you could never refuse Kamal's famous super-moist chocolate cake.

Taverna du Liban was an institution on the Kabul landscape and Kamal had that charming restaurateur's gift of making every patron feel they were his best friend. Hundreds of people found fun and enchantment socializing, discussing business or making deals at his comfortable restaurant, where wine was served in teapots, and where they returned time and again for the best hummus outside of Beirut, and, as far as I am concerned, his globally unrivalled pita.

Kamal and I started to talk the first time about his much-loved cat, a large photo of which hung in the restaurant, overseeing all the goings-on and making sure everything was under control. Kamal mourned his dead moggie in the same way I mourned my childhood dog Oliver, and the little puppy from Kabul, Hilly, that I so wanted to take back to London. Kamal was an old-time communist from Iraq, and he and I also talked about his birthplace, from where I had reported on a number of occasions in 2003 and 2004.

For those of us who were regulars, there are countless anecdotes about times spent at the Taverna. I can't remember all the visits I made, during the day, at night and sometimes in the afternoon, when I'd drop by just to see if Kamal was around for a chat. He would tell me stories about how vodka was brought into the country, and the gangs who controlled the trade and hiked the price. He said he never paid bribes. Perhaps his lavish and legendary generosity protected him.

One time I went there with Karen Woo, Jenner and a Californian friend we called Shakira because of her resemblance to the Colombian pop star. It was shortly before Karen was to leave on her trek and I wanted to talk to Jenner and Shakira about their experiences as contractors of corruption on American bases. It was research for an article

I planned to write about the abuse and shenanigans that went on in the contracting offices.

As we got out of the car, we were confronted by the sight of a young man lying on the ground having an epileptic seizure. Dressed in the shalwar kameez she had bought at the market a few days before, Karen told the men at the scene that she was a doctor. They helped her to put something soft under the man's head and Karen confirmed that he would be fine in a few minutes. Then we went into the Taverna and were greeted by Kamal, who was installed, as always, at his table at the back of the second room – a position that allowed him, like his cat, to oversee events.

We had the premises entirely to ourselves as it was an odd time of day, and we sat outside in the late-afternoon sunshine. We talked about Karen's imminent adventure, which made Jenner so anxious, and also her forthcoming wedding.

This led to talk of weddings in general, and I mentioned how disturbed I had been, after attending a wedding reception recently, to see just how much food was left over – absolutely colossal amounts in a country where food scarcity was a major issue. Weddings in Afghanistan had become more and more ostentatious and extravagant, bankrupting families or throwing them into serious debt.

Enormous wedding halls had started to appear – soulless, cavernous rooms with little charm, illuminated by nasty neon lights, that could accommodate hundreds of people. The outside decorations included glittering Eiffel Towers and row upon row of lights – a kitschy Hanging Gardens of Babylon. Worst of all, though, were the obscene amounts of wasted food.

I asked Kamal what he thought about starting a food bank. It was hardly a radical suggestion, but clearly there had to be ways of distributing the leftover food from restaurants and big events. Kamal organized a trial run and sent some of his staff to the poorer parts of town to dole out what he had left from the restaurant. It ended up being too complicated, though – like so many things in Afghanistan – and Kamal was also rightly concerned that if anyone who had eaten his food fell ill, he would be held responsible.

Nevertheless, Kamal's generosity showed itself in other ways, and my story is, I am sure, just one of hundreds. Before I left in 2011 I asked him to cater my going-away party. The food was duly delivered to my house, but the driver told me Kamal wouldn't take any money for it. I was genuinely horrified – I might have accepted a cake as a gift, but felt terrible taking food for an entire party without paying for it. Desperate to repay Kamal's kindness in some way I hit on an idea for a gift for him – something I loved, and hoped he would love too . . .

Truck art – the elaborate, brightly coloured painting that decorates 'jingle' trucks from Afghanistan and Pakistan – had recently become trendy in Kabul. I had already bought myself a painting of the swan boats on Lake Band-e Amir, which captured the spirit of my favourite place in the country, and I decided to go back to the shop to select something for Kamal. I found a picture of a truck, which I'm happy to say he hung in the Taverna near the photo of his beloved cat.

When Kamal had moved to Lebanon, he had hankered after the edge that life in a place like Kabul brought. But that attraction had begun to fade, he told me, and from what I remember of my conversations with him, I'm not sure how much he loved it there in the end; he tended to stay in his compound and didn't venture out much. He talked to me, and many others, about leaving; he no longer needed that buzz – that thrill. He talked about starting over in other countries. He and I even explored the possibility of opening a restaurant in the UK. I said I would scout out locations, but it never came to anything. That wasn't where my future lay, and probably not Kamal's either.

He never did leave.

Kabul was reasonably safe, even though the parameters of that safety had shrunk over the years, and the ring of steel erected by NATO closed the city in – something that was especially apparent to the old Afghan hands who had known the capital in better days. And despite the goings-on around town, the Taverna had always been deemed safe. Yet Kamal's restaurant morphed almost overnight from one with a large garden that opened out on to the streets of Wazir Akbar Khan into a barricaded fortress, protected by bulletproof doors, guards with guns, escape routes and survival plans.

No one ever thinks it's going to happen to them, or even to someone they know. On the ground everything looks different, for a start; and it feels different too – calmer, normal and certainly more manageable than it appears through the long-distance lens that skews perspective. Only problem: trouble is trouble, and when it does happen, what then?

On 17 January 2014, despite the barricades, the warmth and the welcome, Kamal, along with twenty-one patrons and staff, was killed by a squad dispatched by the Taliban – yet more senseless deaths among the thousands of others over the decade-plus engagement in Afghanistan.

I was in London when the news came through. Another bomb . . . a restaurant . . . foreigners. Was it anyone we knew or any place we used to go? It didn't take long to find out it was the Taverna, and that one of the casualties was Kamal.

A suicide bomber had blown himself up at the front door, killing the guards. Then two gunmen who were already in the restaurant began shooting the people around them. Kamal had his gun, the news reported, and died defending his guests, his staff, his restaurant and himself. It was a bloody siege.

At first, it's the shock that hits you. Then there's the sadness, then the regret that you never really said goodbye, and the realization that you will never see this old friend again. And sometimes, because of the distance, it can seem unreal. That is, until you see the pictures of the mangled buildings and the dead bodies of men and women, Afghan and expat, hiding, trying to save their lives. Then you can smell the fear and see the hate.

When something like this happens, everyone thinks it's the end of an era. Companies put their staff on lockdown, no one is allowed to move, the restaurants empty out and the community hunkers down. In the immediate aftermath of the Taverna's destruction, the UN quarantined its staff, only allowing them to visit other UN compounds – shops and restaurants were off-limits, no exceptions. There are always a few brave souls who venture out as if nothing has happened, though, and then, eventually, things calm down, life returns to normal and everyone forgets about 'the recent unpleasantness'.

This time it feels different, like the last days of the Raj, as we dismantle our final colonial outpost.

21. Clear Hold Build

The first, the supreme, the most far-reaching act of judgment that the statesman and commander have to make is to establish the kind of war on which they are embarking.

Carl von Clausewitz, Prussian general and military historian

It is said that every soldier needs his dead-German quote . . .

Clear Hold – a counterinsurgency strategy developed by the British during the Malayan Emergency

Clear Hold Build – counterinsurgency policy in Afghanistan:

- **Clear** contested ground
- **Hold** to isolate and defend from insurgent influence
- **Build** economic, developmental activity to legitimise counterinsurgency and the government it represents

Small Wars Journals

Causes for War

In modern times wars to defend the innocent are increasing-
ly regarded as just . . . The clearest example of a just cause
is self-defence against an aggressor. For example, when an
enemy has crossed your borders and invaded your territory.
But an actual invasion is not required.

BBC, online ethics guide

First, some questions:

- What was our mission?
- What have we learned?
- Should we have gone to war?
- What has Afghanistan gained?
- Did we have achievable objectives?
- Why did we not walk away after six months?
- Did we understand what we were getting into?
- What was the point if the country returns to the
  way it was before?

Here are some things you need to know about the war-torn
state of Afghanistan.

- In 2014 Afghanistan was ranked the most violent
  country in the world in the Global Peace Index that
  tracks these things. That's one shocking statistic,

given that civil war has consumed Syria, war has broken out in Ukraine, Russia has annexed Crimea, Libya is up in flames and Iraq is once again in turmoil, not to mention the conflict in Mali, Nigeria, South Sudan and the Central African Republic.

- In 2013 209,000 hectares (806 square miles) of poppy were planted across Afghanistan, up 36 per cent on the year before (and the year before that and the year before that). This produced an estimated 5,500 metric tons (6,062 tons) of opium, according to the United Nations drug agency. The 2014 harvest is expected to exceed that record. The industry employs about 200,000 families.

- On 11 September 2001, al-Qaeda, based in Afghanistan, flew two planes into the World Trade Center in Manhattan. This was the first major attack on US territory since the Japanese bombed Pearl Harbor on 7 December 1941, bringing the United States into World War Two. Most countries condemned Osama bin Laden's audacious attack; some said the Americans deserved it. The War on Terror began with the invasion of Afghanistan on 7 October 2001. No one anticipated that the war would last more than a decade.

- The United Nations authorized an international
  military and development presence in Afghanistan
  on 20 December 2001: Security Council
  Resolution 1386 was collectively approved by the
  twenty-eight member countries of the NATO-led
  ISAF mission in Afghanistan. They were there
  at the request and with the approval of
  Afghanistan's new government. Initially ISAF's
  mandate was to provide security in and around
  Kabul, but in October 2003, the UN extended
  this to cover the whole of Afghanistan
  (UNSCR 1510).

What von Clausewitz said in the nineteenth century remains true, and seems to be the central dilemma of the Afghan offensive – if such a complex campaign can be distilled down to one phrase. The goals were not well defined, and there was too little too late.

There was also interference from Pakistan, where the Taliban retreated and regrouped, and other regional powers such as India. There were insufficient forces in the field, a top-heavy command structure at ISAF HQ and myriad other complex, interlinked and separate problems that will occupy historians for decades.

And an overly optimistic timeframe: it was impossible to nation-build in six- or twelve-month rotations, which is what the military mandated. Governments, planning for the short term, didn't heed advice that nothing could be done in three-year bursts. For anything to be established there needed to be a long-term strategy, but there was neither the will nor the desire to commit the necessary resources. Even if nation-building had been possible, it was hugely problematic in such a poor and corrupt country as Afghanistan and would have taken at least a generation. The military had become social workers, civil engineers and nurses, and peacekeeping had become counterinsurgency.

As the situation evolved, some said that the military seemed incapable of developing a strategy that changed with the times; some put it down to arrogance. Ultimately, the solution could not be a military one, as Dan McNeill and many others have observed; only a political and diplomatic solution will work in the long term.

Unsustainable projects were launched, and too much policy was based on erroneous assumptions. One very clear example was the Female Engagement Teams, which became hugely popular and were seen as the foundation of peace. With no clear mandate or power, female soldiers who didn't speak the local language were sent to villages to win the hearts and minds of the womenfolk. The women, having been won over, were then supposed to change the way men thought, so they would support NATO and we could all live happily ever after. Why it was assumed women would think differently is not clear, and as a result Afghan culture was misinterpreted by people who lacked any deep understanding of what they had witnessed.

Then there was support of the wrong people that disillusioned and disheartened 'ordinary' Afghans, who saw vast sums of money go to corrupt officials and very little international aid trickle down to the people it was meant to help.

The return of the warlords to parliament and other positions of power across the country understandably fuelled resentment too. Large amounts of cash were thrown at problems, often exacerbating the situation, but there was never enough to actually solve the fundamental issues.

There were internal strategic contradictions: agencies that didn't speak to each other and departments following different doctrines. And that was just at the US embassy.

According to former US ambassador Karl Eikenberry, writing in *Foreign Affairs*, the American military

> claimed to have a winning plan that it pretended
> was supported by the Afghan head of state and

commander in chief. But this was a complete fiction. Karzai disagreed intellectually, politically and viscerally with the key pillars of the COIN campaign. The result was that while American military commanders tirelessly worked to persuade the Afghan president through factual presentation, deference and occasional humor that the plan was working, they never seemed to consider that Karzai just might not be on board.

Eikenberry's counterpart, General David Petraeus, was the father of COIN, and took 'greatness status' for it. But for many critics it was flawed from the outset because it did not deny insurgents a safe haven. They could and did flee to Pakistan across the open border. The strategy was designed to connect Afghans to their government, which turned out to be more corrupt and almost as vicious as the Taliban, and it was designed to connect key areas of stability, but that depended on governance and development, which the military had planned on rolling out over two years. In Afghanistan, with its extremely low human capital, this was more likely to take fifty.

Iraq and Afghanistan have changed the way we think about war and going to war. Countries like the UK, Canada and the US are now much more hesitant to commit resources, personnel and ideology, as both Iraq and Afghanistan, even a decade on, are arguably no better than they were. So while it may be too early to judge the final result of this last ill-conceived colonial adventure, it has undoubtedly made us all wary of future involvement. And this misadventure, if that is indeed what it turns out to be, is not something that can be laid at the feet of one person. As Dan McNeill said, 'If it's so easy, why doesn't someone do it?'

Clear Hold Build turned out to be more like a can of hairspray than a workable political, military and humanitarian strategy – from this vantage point in time, anyway. Many unanswered questions still remain, not least of which is: how did we get it so terribly wrong?

22. Afterword: Things Fall Apart

It's autumn 2013, and I am sitting in my London flat watching the monsoon-like rain, oppressed by the greyness.

Afghanistan is last year's story. The world is weary of its war and its arcane machinations, its endless struggles and the same old narrative. It has reached the same point I did. I couldn't write the same things about the same issues any more. Not that they stopped being worth writing about, just that someone else had to do it.

It's true that the light isn't as magical here, nor is there that heightened sense of reality. And I don't carry its burdens any more either (not that anyone ever asked me to); I have returned them to their rightful owners.

The backdrop of war, the slow daily drip of adrenalin, the meaning, the clarity, the accomplishment, the fun – they have all disappeared. My journey has taken me a long way from home, way out of my perceived comfort zone. As much as I loved my time in Afghanistan, as much as I loved the country and the people I met, and as much as I wanted to stay, I knew I had to leave. Where did my journey take me? Deeper, perhaps, into an unknown world, close enough to danger to peer in but from a safe enough distance to return unscathed.

It's not only the Taliban who wait. The vultures have circled for a long time, ready to pick at the carcass of broken dreams and hopes, of misbegotten missions and misunderstandings. Former warlords like the Walrus and Hekmatyar, the old enemies, also wait. The same Afghan cast of characters inhabit the same space and still there is no critical mass large enough to force change.

Many of us left disappointed. We had wanted to change the world, or change Afghanistan; maybe just one person's life – maybe even our own. Instead, we went back to our old lives and our old ways, and waited for all the old stuff that always happens to keep happening in Afghanistan – always missing it, never feeling as alive as when we were there.

We dispersed to countries around the globe, to lives disassociated from the past, but connected to each other. We extracted ourselves – Jenner, Benazir, Other Heidi, Debbie, Ariana, Paul, Gracie, me – but we still talk about old times when we meet, of the restaurants and the parties, of the people we knew and of the future that never was.

Jenner languished in Kabul for a few years after I left, always looking for the pot of gold at the end of the rainbow. On Thursday nights you'd find him dancing with cartoon-like charm, falling in love with a new woman and suffering heartbreak and rejection by the break of dawn the next day. In his final months there he sequestered himself at Green Village, an establishment that charged close to US$5,000 a month for a fortified room and high-speed internet.

Jenner planned to slip away and leave Kabul and Afghanistan far behind – to find a new destination where he could recharge his batteries and lick his wounds. Life has a funny way of working out: he booked his ticket, put his three container loads of furniture and treasures in storage and ventured out to one last party where, after years of looking, and having finally said, 'No more', he met her. It was love at first sight and it was mutual. Everything fell into place and he was at peace. Last time we spoke, he was married, with a baby girl whose two doting parents almost never met.

Paul rattled around Helmand and Kandahar for a few more years, then in various conflict zones in Africa before ending up with a woman he had met somewhere en route to somewhere else.

Nathaniel returned to his Antipodean life, lost for ever on the other side of the world.

Dave and Ariana were thrown in jail for the serious crime of sex outside of marriage, the penalty for which is death. But a mystery man – someone who Dave alleged was in the Secret Service and knew of his illustrious reputation – heard about their situation and rushed into action. The man found the US$10,000 the couple needed to bribe their way out of jail, and when I saw them some time later it looked as if Ariana was well on the way to getting what she really wanted. She had a husband, a baby and maybe, most importantly of all, a chance at a new life in a country that wasn't Afghanistan.

Brian got married. He never saw Ariana again.

Dunia and Gracie Belle stayed in touch – Dunia continued to exasperate future employers with great flair, while Gracie moved back to Sydney to be with her son.

In DC, Other Heidi trained diplomats destined for Afghanistan until she was appointed as the political advisor to the head of NATO's Land Command in Izmir, Turkey.

Hasina . . . I cannot say what happened to her. She is always in my thoughts.

And the rabbits. One day they just disappeared. Gracie Belle and I assumed they must have made someone a good meal.

22. AFTERWORD: THINGS FALL APART

The last of the cool kids still ski and still party in Afghanistan. For the rest, it's time to pack up the cappuccino capital and export the adventure to the next war zone.

Acknowledgements

A number of people have made a huge impact on my life and these include Heather Grace Jones, Heidi Meyer, Mark Smith, Kate Fox, Frank Ledwidge, Sandy Fainer, Yvonne Ndege, Moa Roshanfar, and all my Kabul friends. I also want to thank my agent, Robert Smith, for his perseverance, my editor, Anne Newman, for her magical skills, Dotti Irving for introducing me to Hector Macdonald, and Hector for his belief in *Dispatches* and me. Finally, thank you to Advance Editions contributors Jon Duschinsky, Marion Molteno, Terry, Georgia Summers, Chris Baker, Heidi Meyer, Monika Kispal, David Willers, Harry W and Hector Macdonald.

For news from Heidi Kingstone, visit
www.HeidiKingstone.com